» CRU «
OYSTER BAR
NANTUCKET
COOKBOOK

» CRU «
OYSTER BAR
NANTUCKET
COOKBOOK

SAVORING FOUR SEASONS
OF THE GOOD LIFE

ERIN ZIRCHER, CRU EXECUTIVE CHEF AND PROPRIETOR
JANE STODDARD, PROPRIETOR
CARLOS HIDALGO, PROPRIETOR

WITH MARTHA W. MURPHY

FOREWORD BY LULU POWERS
PHOTOGRAPHS BY WAYNE CHINNOCK

ST. MARTIN'S GRIFFIN
NEW YORK

www.stmartins.com

Photographs by Wayne Chinnock

Design by: Rita Sowins / Sowins Design

The Library of Congress Cataloging-in-Publication Data is available upon request.

ISBN 978-1-250-19365-0 (hardcover)
ISBN 978-1-250-19366-7 (ebook)

Our books may be purchased in bulk for promotional, educational, or business use. Please contact your local bookseller or the Macmillan Corporate and Premium Sales Department at 1-800-221-7945, extension 5442, or by email at MacmillanSpecialMarkets@macmillan.com.

First Edition: May 2019

10 9 8 7 6 5 4 3 2 1

TO OUR TREMENDOUSLY LOYAL GUESTS:

YOU HAVE BEEN INVALUABLE IN SHAPING
THE CRU EXPERIENCE AS IT IS TODAY.
THANK YOU FOR CONTINUOUSLY INSPIRING US
SEASON AFTER SEASON.

CONTENTS

FOREWORD

LULU POWERS

"SOMETIMES YOU WANT TO GO
WHERE EVERYBODY KNOWS YOUR NAME
AND THEY'RE ALWAYS GLAD YOU CAME . . .
YOU WANT TO BE . . ."
AT CRU OYSTER BAR NANTUCKET HARBOR.

Walking into CRU is like coming home, whether it's your first time there or your hundredth. Sure it's the place, but it's really the people, a charming cast of characters that make this little "gin joint" sing. First there is Sweet Jane, the consummate hostess who runs CRU like a ship captain but is smiling no matter what. Carlos, Mr. Jazzamarazz, fills the room with his singular flair and sports the most wonderful pocket squares! Erin, the chef and consummate creative, is always whipping up something delicious and unforgettable. And finally Tommy, aka "my boyfriend," who makes the best "Sneeky" in town at the back bar. Regulars and newcomers alike are treated like part of the gang, just spend five minutes at the back bar and you'll see. CRU is one big happy family where everyone really does know your name.

Then of course there is the food. You can't leave without trying my favorites: the crispy calamari with harissa aioli and a CRUcomber cocktail. Who knew cucumbers and lemon balm could rise to new heights together? Also, CRU's hot buttered lobster roll on toasted brioche is in another league, which is saying a lot on Nantucket, where lobster rolls abound. And for dessert, grab a spoonful of the butterscotch dessert on your way out. Yum!

My favorite spot at CRU is the back bar at the end of Straight Wharf. When I was growing up, my family would gather there after Sunday mass, making new friends and memories over the perfect clam chowder. Later in the day, the sound of magnums popping over the chatter of the full crowd with the cool breeze coming in off the water is simply heaven. It's what I think of when I'm missing our faraway island and the people there I love. It is what always brings me back, like a song.

So whether you're coming back or arriving on Nantucket for the first time, head straight to CRU and join the gang in the front room, back bar, or right on Straight Wharf. And don't forget to keep a CRU cookbook, for the moments when you're missing great friends and food. Just open it to any page and your table, along with a friendly smile, will be waiting.

INTRODUCTION

WELCOME TO
CRU OYSTER BAR
NANTUCKET,
WELCOME TO THE ISLAND

Stroll down Straight Wharf and you will discover our restaurant, CRU Oyster Bar Nantucket, sitting directly on the waterfront of beautiful Nantucket Harbor; turn and look 180 degrees in the other direction and you'll be facing handsome historic downtown Nantucket. The iconic island address of One Straight Wharf has a history as old as the town's. As you approach, we think you'll find CRU's exterior to be pretty, but unassuming; clad in cedar shingles weathered to a silvery gray, accented with white trim, CRU looks like so many other classic Nantucket buildings. But step inside and you'll find an interior that is as elegant and sleek as the yachts moored just beyond our windows. From our intimate, chic dining rooms, boisterous back bar, and waterfront deck, our guests enjoy unobstructed views of the harbor and, beyond it, Nantucket Sound. According to publications like *Travel + Leisure*, *The New York Times*, *Saveur*, and *The Wall Street Journal* among others, they also enjoy superlative food and cocktails, including the island's best raw bar.

While our name might imply that CRU is a raw bar only—that feature is considered by many to be our hallmark—CRU is a full-fledged restaurant with an award-winning wine list, inventive cocktails, and French-influenced approach to local seafood and produce.

To us, however, CRU is more than what reviewers have praised as an "unparalleled" raw bar and "chic, expertly run restaurant." It is a place where we do our best every day to present not only exquisite food prepared from the finest ingredients,

superb wines and cocktails, and exceptional service, but also where we strive to offer a unique experience that is worthy of our guests and worthy of this magical place called Nantucket.

In this book, we are sharing—for the very first time—recipes for some of CRU's offerings. Deciding which ones to include was difficult! In the end, we gathered a selection that reflects a sampling of our guests' favorites as well as our own. From rustic picnic fare to elegant dishes that call for a bottle of Pol Roger champagne, we believe this collection reflects the understated elegance and restrained sophistication that is the essence of our style—and of Nantucket itself.

As you'll see, the recipes are arranged to follow the seasons, chapter by chapter, and reflect the island's bounty from early spring through the late fall. That said, each of us makes a point of traveling every year during the months CRU is closed to explore food

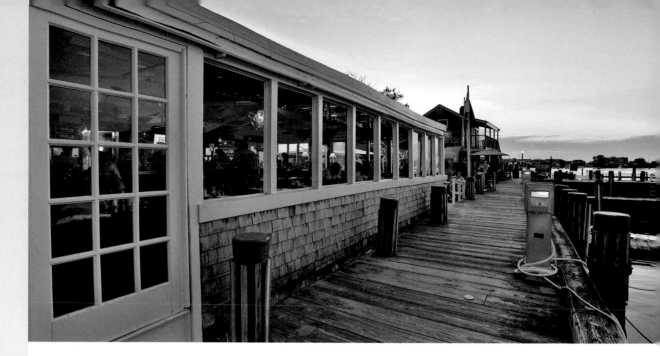

and wine in other parts of the world. So you will taste influences from far-flung destinations, too.

The waters around Nantucket are the source of some of the world's best seafood. Those delicacies have been the inspiration for our menu since we opened CRU: you'll find within these pages recipes for Fluke Meunière; Harissa Grilled Tuna with Leeks Vinaigrette; Crispy Fried Oysters with Bibb Lettuce and Radish Rémoulade; and Crudo of Nantucket Bay Scallops with Ginger Mignonette and Pear, to name a handful. Recipes for Grilled Lobsters with Herb and Coral Butter; Lobster Rolls; Pernod-spiked Lobster Bisque; Lobster Salad with Grapefruit, Avocado, and Quinoa; and Lobster Cocktail with citrus and tarragon are included here, too.

You'll discover far more in this book than dishes that highlight fish and shellfish: enjoy the recipe for Turkish-inspired Spiced Fried Chicken; Confit-Style Duck Legs; a Warm Farro Salad with Walnuts and Kale; a French-inspired Potato Salad with Capers and Soft-Cooked Eggs; Zucchini Ribbon Salad with Lemon Vinaigrette and Mint; a savory Heirloom Tomato Tart; a classic Creamy Cucumber Salad; and the *best* sandwiches you'll ever pack for a day at the beach.

And then there are the desserts. Inspired by family recipes as well as Erin's reinterpretation of the classics, you'll find recipes here for out-of-this-world cookies, simple cakes made special with fresh fruit, and pies that can be made in jars for a picnic. Where to begin

"FROM OUR INTIMATE, CHIC DINING ROOMS, BOISTEROUS BACK BAR, AND WATERFRONT DECK, OUR GUESTS ENJOY UNOBSTRUCTED VIEWS OF THE HARBOR AND, BEYOND IT, NANTUCKET SOUND."

might be your biggest challenge. Should it be Hazelnut Shortbread with Wild Blackberry Jam; Vanilla-Rum Grilled Plums with Orange-Scented Pound Cake; or sea salted Chocolate Pots de Crème? We think it will be difficult to decide . . .

At CRU, we believe there is a wine for every palate. Our list is primarily composed of old-world wines, focusing on the best examples from every region. Toast your evening with one of our unique-grower champagnes, highlighting one of the most vibrant regions in the heart of France. Take a trip up the California coastline and experience the many ways fog, terroir, and altitude can express themselves, whether in a robust Cabernet or a mouth-watering rosé. The soul of our wine list lies in Burgundy, where our selection of Chardonnays and Pinot Noirs pairs perfectly with the coastal cuisine that defines CRU.

Inventive cocktails, as pretty as they are delicious, are collected here in a chapter of recipes for seasonally appropriate drinks as well as ones that qualify as any-time go-to favorites. Whether you're hosting a brunch, a cocktail party, or a holiday get-together, these concoctions are bound to improve your status as a host.

You'll find variety in this book: dishes you can make in advance, recipes for the grill, elegant hors d'oeuvres, and cocktails that can elevate any gathering. We have put together menus to suit diverse entertaining styles and to inspire you throughout the year. Whatever your palate, we hope you'll enjoy cooking from these recipes and, better yet, sharing the results with family and friends.

We also hope you'll find that thumbing through this book is like visiting the island. We wanted to bring you—in words and in pictures—a sense of what makes Nantucket so special. From its stunning natural beauty to its eclectic mix of residents to its world-class shops, galleries, and hotels, the island casts a mesmerizing spell.

We thought and talked about sharing these stories and recipes in a book for a long time. Now that it's done, we can see it's really more than a cookbook or lifestyle-and-travel guide. It's a love letter—to the guests who have helped make CRU Oyster Bar Nantucket a beloved place, to those who provide us with exquisite ingredients for the food we serve, and to Nantucket itself. *Thank you*, CRU fans and guests. *Thank you*, farmers and fishermen. And *thank you*, Universe, for bringing us to this faraway, windswept, magical place.

Wherever you are as you read this book: we hope you love CRU as much as we do! Cheers!

Erin Zircher
Jane Stoddard
Carlos Hidalgo

MEET THE
CRU CREW

THE TRIO THAT
FOUNDED THE PLACE
TO BE ON
NANTUCKET

When we each arrived on the island of Nantucket, it was during different years and at different points in our lives. We did not know one another, nor did any one of us know we would stay and make the island home. And we certainly did not know we would one day share a business.

Sometimes the stars align and that certainly seemed true for us. We each had skills that would make us, as a trio, ideal partners in a restaurant. Erin's classical French training and fondness for Mediterranean flavors suited the simple yet innovative cuisine we all loved—and believed would be the foundation of an exceptional seafood restaurant. Her experience in noted kitchens ranging from Chicago and France to Boston and Cambridge gave her an exceptional foundation for a project of this scale. That background, plus her dedication to seasonal farm-to-table menus, made her a sought-after talent.

Jane's passion and experience was in restaurant operations. Her résumé included the elite roles of general manager and director of operations while at premier Nantucket restaurants. Her attention to detail, tireless energy, and ability to hire, train, and coach a staff of diverse individuals into a cohesive enthusiastic team would be integral to the success of any restaurant, particularly one that would attract a discerning clientele.

Carlos brought a separate set of skills and expertise to the group. His education (a degree in hospitality administration from Boston University) had opened doors where his talent was quickly recognized, leading to roles as restaurant manager in multiple venues in both Boston and on Nantucket. His passion for and knowledge of wines and spirits added yet another reason he would make an ideal partner.

Our shared love of travel with a focus on exploring food and wine in other parts of the world became an instant connection. Living and working on an island with an "off season" had given each of us the opportunity to make annual culinary trips a tradition. Our common philosophy was (and is) that keeping our knowledge of food and wine up to date, and expansive, was essential to being able to offer guests an exceptional dining experience.

When an opportunity to make our dream a reality came along in the form of an ideally located waterfront building, we took the leap. Beautifully situated but in need of a makeover, the structure at One Straight Wharf had to be completely renovated and redesigned. Our goal: a glamorous space and welcoming vibe where guests would be equally comfortable coming straight from their boats or dressed for a celebratory night on the town. We chose the Boston-based interior design firm Gauthier-Stacy to help us get there. It was a wonderfully collaborative process and the outcome was the perfect balance of casual elegance and rustic luxury.

CRU Oyster Bar Nantucket takes its name from the French word *cru*, which has several meanings, one of which is "raw," as in *poisson cru* (raw fish). The word also designates a top-quality vineyard whose wines reveal the unique flavors of the location—fitting, we thought, for a restaurant where a curated wine list complements cuisine that celebrates its coastal setting. The name is also a play on words for "crew" and, as we often point out, the nautical reference to a tight-knit team is exactly right for our restaurant. We are proud of our CRU crew, as they are essential to the warm, welcoming vibe and reflect our core mission of providing our guests with smart, genuine, intuitive hospitality.

Since opening in May 2012, CRU has earned a reputation as a culinary destination unmatched on Nantucket. We have been honored by praise that notes our raw bar as offering the most expansive selection on the island; our exceptionally pristine seafood; and our award-winning wine and cocktail menu. Our goal remains the same as the day we opened CRU: that our ocean-inspired menu, beautiful dining rooms, and stunning waterfront views will continue to embody the laid-back but elegant Nantucket lifestyle.

WHY WE LOVE OUR "FARAWAY ISLAND"

National Geographic calls Nantucket the "best island in the world." The Nature Conservancy cites it as "one of the last great places on earth." And everyone who lives or visits here describes the island as "magical." We agree.

With nearly 50 percent of the island protected as open space and held in conservation by several land trust organizations, these accolades are no surprise.

But there's something else that sets Nantucket apart and makes the highly coveted luxe lifestyle here unique. It can only be described as a vibe created by a place that is

- laid-back but elegant,
- remote but contemporary,
- exclusive but not pretentious, and
- luxe, despite its rustic characteristics.

Those who arrive by boat are delivered to what qualifies as the prettiest harbor in New England, facing the historic district of downtown Nantucket. Lining its cobblestone streets and brick-paved sidewalks is an unparalleled collection of beautifully maintained Georgian, Federal, and Greek Revival buildings, home to chic high-end shops of exclusive artisan items; art galleries; antiques stores; and charming cafés—buzzing with an international crowd.

Bumping up against the town and easily accessible, Nantucket's natural beauty mesmerizes; the eighty-plus miles of soft-sand soul-renewing beaches, wide stretches of dunes, and masses of wild roses make a lasting impression. But there are also moors, forests, grasslands, and cranberry bogs. More than 350 kinds of birds visit the island each summer, many of them rare species not readily found elsewhere in the United States.

And then there's the light. Lying thirty miles off the southern coast of Cape Cod, the island is bathed in a glow reflected off the sea that surrounds it. Luminous, remote, inviting: Nantucket enchants the mind.

On this faraway, windswept, unique place, the island's artists, farmers, commercial fishermen, shopkeepers, designers, entrepreneurs, and billionaires commingle with ease, as effortlessly as the lobster boats and world-class yachts share its harbor. The easy camaraderie, the island's incredible natural beauty, and its understated luxury create a lifestyle that is the essence of Nantucket's magic.

A BRIEF HISTORY OF NANTUCKET

The first inhabitants of Nantucket were the Wampanoag, native Americans whose legacy includes the island's name, meaning "faraway island." In the 1640s, the British began establishing settlements on the island, attracted to the rich fishing grounds off its shores.

Finfish like cod were plentiful and the process of preserving it made it quite valuable. Salt cod became so popular in Europe that fortunes were built on it. (Historians claim that profits from the lucrative salt cod trade were a significant source of funding for the American Revolution.) Salt cod was considered more delicious than fresh cod in the eighteenth century (a surprise to today's tastes), so fishmongers would refer to fresh cod as "fresh salt cod" to increase its appeal to shoppers!

The English settlers also found the island ideal for raising sheep; small-scale carding and spinning enterprises on the island fed the wool market in the colonies, where wool was a thriving industry. But it was whaling that put Nantucket "on the map." The Wampanoags and the English knew whales traveled the waters off the island; a whale would occasionally wash ashore. By the 1690s, Nantucket fishermen were going out in small boats to hunt for them and by 1715, deep-sea whaling had begun. By the mid-eighteenth century, large whaleships that could go to sea for a year (or three or four or five) were pulling in and out of Nantucket regularly, and everything associated with the whaling business—from outfitting the ships to processing the whale oil—made Nantucket a very wealthy community. Nantucket was the busiest whaling port on the globe and was referred to as the "whaling capital of the world."

In its heyday whaling looked like a business that could go on forever, but by the 1830s it was coming to an end as whale oil was replaced by petroleum from oil fields in Pennsylvania. Extracting oil from the ground was about to become the next big thing, and whaling—along with a way of life for many Nantucketers—would come to an end.

But by then, Nantucket had been "discovered" as a wonderful place for off-islanders to get away from it all. The restorative benefits of "sea-bathing" on Nantucket were extolled in newspapers and, as a result, small inns and rooming houses were doing well. By the 1870s, the demand for accommodations on the island was so great that large elegant summer hotels were built, marking the beginning of Nantucket's reputation as a world-class vacation destination. The first vacationers were mostly from Boston and New York City but today, visitors from around the world make their way to Nantucket—for its fine "sea-bathing," world-class blue water sailing, exquisite dining and shopping, and understated luxe lifestyle.

RAW BAR BASICS

A DELICIOUS BALANCING ACT

CRU

Oyster Bar Nantucket is renowned for its raw bar. The pristine quality and substantial selection of fresh oysters (our menu features eight to a dozen different varieties daily) and hard-shell clams are why CRU's raw bar is considered the most expansive on the island. Beautifully displayed on beds of crushed ice, everything is expertly shucked to order (never in advance!), and impeccably served with a variety of handmade cocktail sauces and plump wedges of lemon.

Another signature offering at CRU, and unique to the Nantucket food scene: our lavish, chilled seafood towers overflowing with tiers of briny oysters and clams, crudos of local fish, Nantucket scallops on the half shell (when they are available for harvest), and tins of the world's best caviars—hand selected in collaboration with Calvisius caviar.

To complete the raw bar menu, CRU offers a variety of chilled shellfish cocktails: blue crab, lobster, and wild-caught shrimp—all beautifully presented and accompanied by the perfect sauce.

Now, with the recipes in this chapter, you can create a memorable evening with your own raw bar. We recommend including a selection of cooked, chilled shellfish—shrimp, crab, or lobster—with the raw items. Crab claws, whole shrimp, or lobster tails halved down the center are delicious, easy choices. Or, you can re-create a couple of CRU's signature seafood cocktails; check out the recipes that appear later in this chapter.

The sauces you'll use with seafood cocktails are the same ones you'll set out to accompany the raw oysters and clams on the half shell. This chapter gives you recipes for four delicious, simple-to-make but out-of-the-ordinary-tasting cocktail sauces, plus serving suggestions.

PREPARING YOUR RAW BAR

Ideally, you'll have a partner helping you shuck. Place each shucked oyster or clam, as you go, immediately on a platter of crushed ice. In advance, set out lots of wedges of juicy lemons and dishes of two or more of CRU's distinctive sauces so that as soon as the shucking is done you can wash your hands and serve.

CHEERS! THE BEST SPIRITS TO SERVE WITH YOUR RAW BAR DELICACIES

Our top pick for a white wine is **Christian Moreau Chablis**. We love its crisp, clean feel in the mouth, its mineral notes, and its acidity. Refreshing but possessing a complexity worthy of oysters on the half shell, this Chablis from a renowned vineyard in France is one of the reasons the wine list at CRU wins awards every year.

Another white wine we love, **Clos Mireille** (from Domaines Ott, a house that produces some of the world's most prestigious wines, and a favorite of ours), will complement the ocean flavors of oysters and the other items at your raw bar. From its delicate, fruity nose of white peach and apricot mixed with passion fruit and mango to its fresh, crisp, full taste, this wine is a perfect match for the salinity and melon tones of our Fifth Bend Nantucket oysters.

For a rosé, **Château de Selle** (also a Domaines Ott wine) is crisp yet uniquely soft, with notes of citrus fruit and orchard flowers. This wine pairs beautifully with our award-winning Crab Cocktail.

A dry champagne, like **Pol Roger**, is another excellent accompaniment.

In addition to offering your guests wine or champagne, a classic gin martini with a lemon twist, icy cold, served straight-up, is a great choice. The distinct bite of gin and dry vermouth makes an excellent accompaniment to the delicate but rich flavors of oysters, clams, and seafood cocktails.

RECIPES FOR

RAW BAR BASICS

OUR TWO FAVORITE NANTUCKET OYSTER FARMERS: STEVE BENDER AND SIMON EDWARDS

At CRU, we serve two locally raised oysters: Pocomo Meadows oysters, grown by Steve Bender, and Fifth Bend oysters, grown by Simon Edwards. Pocomo Meadows oysters are grown in the mouth of Polpis Harbor, near two fresh-water creeks, which lends a sweet mineral taste to them. Fifth Bends are grown in the head of Nantucket Harbor in deep water, giving them a wonderful briny flavor. Steve and Simon provide us with these exquisite oysters every day, for our entire CRU season. We consider their high-quality locally grown oysters to be the cornerstone of our raw bar.

MEET: STEVE BENDER—SCIENTIST, ENTREPRENEUR, AND OYSTER FARMER

Oyster farming is Steve Bender's ninth career. A chemist by training, with degrees

from Alfred, Columbia, and MIT, he has traveled the world including as an invited lecturer in Japan and Russia. Although he was raised in the Bronx, he has now lived on the island for enough years to call himself a longtime Nantucket resident.

Describing himself as "lucky," he says he "happened to hit a couple of home runs in research," which meant that in 1970 when a friend mentioned there was a restaurant for sale on Nantucket, Steve (who had never even visited the island) checked it out and bought it. He enjoyed the restaurant business but seven years later was ready to sell. He stayed on the island, though, had a boat built and went fishing for cod and tuna; during the winter, he often went scalloping.

The genesis of his start in oyster farming came about when he took a course in aquaculture offered by FEMA in the early 1980s. He was intrigued but, at that time, there were no places left to raise oysters on the island. In 2008, when the opportunity to purchase rights to farm oysters in the waters at the mouth of Polpis Harbor became available—which he had been actively pursuing for years—he jumped at it.

Steve farms sub-tidally in an eight-acre fresh and saltwater estuary, Pocomo Meadows, with his wife, Anna Lynn, and their son, Emil. It's a seven-day-a-week job most of the year, and days are long, but he loves the work and wouldn't trade it for anything. "The setting is gorgeous. The oysters are incredible." Fans agree. Delicate but complex, with a distinct mineral flavor.

When he's not farming, Steve is advocating for protection of Nantucket Harbor and the surrounding environment.

Steve's favorite way to enjoy oysters? Raw, on the half shell. He notes that the flavor varies quite a bit throughout the season. To him, the oysters are most delicious during late spring/early summer, and all through the fall. For those who prefer oysters that have been cooked, Steve recommends oysters Rockefeller as the best way to go and will even share his recipe with you if you catch him in the off-season.

When asked if a background in chemistry comes in handy for an oyster farmer, Steve looks incredulous. "Chemistry comes in handy in everyday *life*!"

MEET: SIMON EDWARDS—WORLD TRAVELER, SCIENTIST, AND OYSTER FARMER

Although he earned a bachelor's degree in biology and a master's degree in aquaculture, Simon Edwards came to oyster farming via a circuitous route. Born and raised in Kenya, he attended university in England and Scotland, after which he lived and worked in Costa Rica for fourteen years. In 2004, he and his wife (a native New Englander) moved to Nantucket.

In 2011, he received the permits to farm oysters in an area he leases at the head of Nantucket Harbor, and found a "perfect occupation." He loves "the freedom, being on the water, growing something, seeing things to completion—the whole thing."

His season starts mid-April and ends in December. Like any kind of farming, it's a seven-day-a-week job most of the year, and weather dictates what can be done as well

as what must be done. During the summer months, he employs help and keeps a crew of up to four busy during the peak season.

There's still plenty to do in the off-season. Besides spending more time with his wife and their three young children, there's pa perwork to attend to, articles to read about advances in oyster farming techniques, and "seed" must be ordered. Simon buys his seed from hatcheries in Maine. "They come overnight in this expensive little box," he explains. "They're so tiny. Two millimeters; that's literally a pencil point."

All the oysters Simon raises are sold on Nantucket. In addition to supplying CRU with fresh oysters daily, he sells to a fish market. But the Fifth Bends he raises are an exclusive to CRU. "The Fifth Bends are grown in the head of Nantucket Harbor in floating cages in deep water, which means plenty of food source. These oysters are plump, meaty and briny."

CREATING A RAW BAR FOR YOUR GUESTS

- Plan on four to six oysters and three to five littlenecks per person.
- Include Crab Cocktail (see page 33) or crab claws, cooked shrimp or Shrimp Cocktail (see page 28), and/or lobster (tails split lengthwise, or lobster cocktail) with the iced oysters and clams on the half shell.
- Prepare one cooked seafood item as a cocktail and present the others in a different form so that your raw bar offers as much variety as possible.
- Make at least three different cocktail sauces to accompany the seafood (this chapter contains four recipes), purchase the plumpest lemons you can find, and be sure to have sufficient wine and champagne thoroughly chilled.

OUR FAVORITE WHITE WINE: CHRISTIAN MOREAU PÈRE ET FILS CHABLIS

Since 1814, the Moreau family has called the region of Chablis, France, home. Today, the Christian Moreau Père et Fils vineyard is located in the centuries-old village of Chablis, set in the heart of the picturesque Chablis countryside on the bank of the Serein River with a south/southeast exposure. The family's winemaking operations sit at the foot of its famous grand cru vineyards there.

The region of Chablis constitutes the northernmost wine district in Burgundy, a renowned wine-making region of France. Because of the cooler temperatures in Chablis, its white wines made from Chardonnay grapes are crisper and more acidic than wines made from Chardonnay grapes grown in warmer climates.

The region's soil (the vineyard's terroir) also contributes to the wine's distinct aroma, beautiful pale-yellow color, and complex taste. All the Chablis region's grand cru vineyards and premier cru vineyards—including Christian Moreau Père et Fils—are planted in an ancient soil composed of limestone, clay, and fossilized oyster shells. (That's right: oyster shells.)

At Christian Moreau Père et Fils, grapes are harvested by hand and the family is committed to organic farming. "Our family is keeping alive a tradition that has lasted for six generations," Fabien Moreau explains. "This means respecting the Chablis' vineyard terroir, the only one of its kind in the world."

One of the oldest and most respected names in Chablis, the Moreau family's exceptional vineyard sites, old vines, and brilliant winemaking techniques produce wines that are regarded as among the best produced in the region. We find that its mineral notes and acidity give it a crisp, refreshing complexity and make it a perfect complement for oysters on the half shell.

CLASSIC COCKTAIL SAUCE

→ MAKES ABOUT 1 CUP ←

If you like horseradish, you'll really like our cocktail sauce. This is the classic we all know and love, with a little extra punch. Delicious with oysters and clams on the half shell, it's also wonderful in a crab or shrimp cocktail.

INGREDIENTS

½ cup prepared horseradish
½ cup ketchup
1 teaspoon Worcestershire sauce
1 tablespoon fresh lemon juice

Combine all the ingredients thoroughly. Transfer to a glass jar with a tight-fitting lid and refrigerate until completely chilled before serving. Can be stored in the refrigerator for up to 1 week.

HORSERADISH CRÈME FRAÎCHE

→ MAKES ABOUT 1 CUP ←

This sauce is incredibly versatile. We serve it with potato pancakes, on top of our smoked salmon tartine, and most importantly, as the very special second sauce in our crab cocktail.

INGREDIENTS

2 ounces cream cheese, room temperature
½ cup crème fraîche
2 tablespoons heavy cream

¼ cup prepared horseradish
½ teaspoon kosher salt
¼ teaspoon freshly ground black pepper

Using a mixer with the whisk attachment, whip the cream cheese until it is completely smooth. Add the crème fraîche and heavy cream and whip on medium-high speed until light and fluffy. Stir in the horseradish, salt, and pepper. Refrigerate until ready to use. Can be stored in the refrigerator for up to 1 week.

MIGNONETTE

There are a million different versions of mignonette out there, but I prefer some things to remain just the way I remember having them for the first time. This is one of those recipes. Perfect with oysters on the half shell; you need only a very small amount with your oyster.

INGREDIENTS

½ cup red wine vinegar
2 shallots, finely minced (¼ cup)
½ teaspoon sugar
¼ teaspoon kosher salt
Freshly ground black pepper

In a small bowl, thoroughly combine the vinegar, shallots, sugar, and salt and season with pepper. Transfer to a glass jar with a tight-fitting lid and refrigerate until completely chilled before serving. Can be stored in the refrigerator for up to 1 week.

KEY LIME DIJONNAISE

Warm weather and sunshine aren't the only perks to spending winter in South Florida: stone crab season occurs from mid-October through mid-May.

The traditional sauce for stone crab seems bizarre to me; it just shouldn't work with the crab, but somehow it really does.

We make Key Lime Dijonnaise for the holiday season when we are lucky enough to score a few pounds of stone crab for the raw bar, but you'll find the sauce is a great addition to any chilled crab presentation.

INGREDIENTS

1 cup Dijon mustard
1 cup mayonnaise
½ cup fresh Key lime or regular lime juice
½ teaspoon kosher salt
Tabasco (optional)

In a medium bowl, thoroughly combine the mustard, mayonnaise, lime juice, and salt and season with Tabasco (if using). Transfer to a glass jar with a tight-fitting lid and refrigerate until ready to serve. Can be stored in the refrigerator for up to 1 week.

SHRIMP COCKTAIL

This cooking technique is my favorite way to prepare shrimp to eat out-of-hand. It's super-easy and foolproof. And because they are cooked so gently, the shrimp are never tough or rubbery.

INGREDIENTS

1 teaspoon sea salt

1 teaspoon whole coriander seeds

1 bay leaf

2 lemon slices

1 pound extra jumbo shrimp (U-15), peeled and deveined

Combine the salt, coriander seeds, bay leaf, and lemon slices in a medium saucepan, add 6 cups water, and bring to a boil over high heat. Add the shrimp and immediately remove the pot from the heat. Let the shrimp sit in the water for 5 minutes (8 minutes if you are using a large shrimp, size U-8).

Remove 1 shrimp and cut in half; it should be just cooked through (if not, set the timer for 1 minute and check again).

Remove the cooked shrimp from the water with a slotted spoon and transfer to a plate to cool. Chill until ready to serve.

The raw bar at CRU is considered by many to be the restaurant's signature, the place where fans don't mind standing shoulder-to-shoulder, three-deep at the bar waiting for their turn to order. Overseeing it all is Rick Sorocco, better known as Rocco, responsible not only for every detail of the operation but also for its fun vibe.

"I love talking with the customers. My guys and I work facing them and it's like being on stage. We're always educating newcomers, talking about the different oysters we're offering that day, making suggestions."

All of CRU's raw bar items are shucked to order, never in advance, which means the shuckers need to be quick. How quick? CRU serves more than 200,000 oysters on the half shell per year (actually, the restaurant is only open May through October, a brief six months), so Rocco selects and trains his crew well. "Most have been working with me for three or four years. They come back every season because they love what they do."

SHUCKING AMAZING

Still, Rocco remains the "master shucker," a title bestowed by CRU's partners—Jane, Erin, and Carlos—during the restaurant's second season, in awe of his amazing prowess. Customers agree, returning as much for the pleasure of hanging out with Rocco as for the unparalleled offerings of the raw bar. The fact that he personally opens thousands of oysters every season—all while welcoming customers, answering questions, and making everyone feel like they've just stepped into the best party on the island—continually confirms his status. He does it all with style and grace, exactly what you'd expect from a former Eagle Scout.

He's had a lifetime of training for his role; as a boy growing up on Nantucket, Rocco went clamming every chance he got, and at age ten, his dad said, "It's time for you to learn how to shuck these yourself."

The island was the perfect childhood home for someone who likes the natural world as much as Rocco. "I like to bike, being outside, the beach, sailing, digging my own clams, fishing. I even thought about being a park ranger for a while." Nowadays, when CRU closes for the season, he spends two months fishing commercially for Nantucket Bay scallops.

Like CRU's three founders, Rocco loves to travel during the off-season and has spent quite a bit of time in Japan, where he finds the food "inspiring," giving him ideas to share with Chef Erin.

ROCCO'S RULES

For those who ask, Rocco gives tips on how to shuck oysters and clams at home: "Take it slow. Always protect your hand with a folded towel or glove—oyster shells are razor-sharp, and the shucking knife can slip and hurt your hand, too."

Other tips: "An oyster has one adductor muscle so open it at its back, at the hinge. A clam has two adductor muscles, so you go in through the front, working the knife under the meat and to the hinge."

Best way to eat an oyster: "First, sip the liquor, then pop the oyster in your mouth and chew a bit before you swallow it. Eat the first one unadorned to get the full spectrum of its flavors, then add lemon, black pepper, cocktail sauce—whatever you like—to the next."

THE BEST JOB, THE PERFECT PLACE TO BE

"One of the things I love about oysters is that, like wine, they can have completely different flavor profiles even when they come from the same region. Nantucket oysters from deep water at the head of the harbor are briny, oceany, while those from Polpis Creek have more minerality and are slightly sweeter." With eight to ten different oysters offered a day, Rocco encourages trying a platter with two of each.

To put in twelve-hour days, seven days a week, six months of the year at CRU takes commitment and passion. Rocco has both in spades. He's exactly where he wants to be and considers himself lucky. "I love it. I have a beautiful 'office' with a view of the harbor. I get to ride my bike to work every day. It's just serenity."

CRAB COCKTAIL

This dish is a favorite at CRU. The inspiration for it comes from a very unlikely place: the Midwest. I was at my grandmother's seventy-fifth birthday celebration in north-central Wisconsin and someone had brought a crab dip to the party. It was simply cream cheese spread on a plate topped with cocktail sauce and canned crabmeat. I couldn't tear myself away from it and have never forgotten tasting it for the first time. I've tried to elevate the recipe a bit with the crème fraîche and super high-quality lump crabmeat, but those classic flavors are all still there.

INGREDIENTS

1 pound jumbo lump crabmeat
1 tablespoon finely chopped fresh chives
1 teaspoon olive oil
¼ cup Horseradish Crème Fraîche (page 25)
¼ cup Classic Cocktail Sauce (page 25)
Flake sea salt
1 lemon, cut into 4 wedges

In a medium bowl, gently toss the crab with the chives and oil. Place 1 tablespoon Horseradish Crème Fraîche in the bottom of each of four small bowls or rocks glasses. Top each with 1 tablespoon Classic Cocktail Sauce, then divide the crab among the bowls. Top with a pinch of flake sea salt and serve each with a wedge of lemon.

DAFFODILS AND ANTIQUE CARS

WELCOMING SPRING, NANTUCKET-STYLE

RECIPES FOR

DAFFODILS AND
ANTIQUE CARS

Nantucket Clam Chowder

Lobster Rolls

Oyster Crackers with Cracked
Fennel Seeds

Spiced Fried Chicken

Potato Salad with Capers and
Soft-Cooked Eggs

Bittersweet Chocolate Whoopie Pies
with Sea-Salt Buttercream

From early April to mid-May, Nantucket is blanketed in yellow as its roadsides, gardens, and window boxes bloom with daffodils. Forty-three years ago, inspired by this quintessential sign of the season and eager to "banish the winter doldrums and welcome spring," the island's Chamber of Commerce began what has been a lively annual tradition during the last weekend of April ever since: The Daffodil Festival of Nantucket.

The weekend's events begin first thing on a Friday and run almost nonstop through Saturday and Sunday. Each day is jam-packed with activities: house and garden tours; a Children's Parade where daffodil-decorated strollers, wagons, and bicycles are shown off; the Daffy Dog Parade where canine friends are decked out in garlands, jaunty chapeaus, and any other garb a good dog can tolerate. There are art shows, the Daffodil 5K Race, and lots of contests—the Daffy Hat contest, Best Window-Box contest, Fifty Shades of Nantucket history quiz contest, and on and on.

A highlight of the Daffodil Festival and a fun-for-all-ages event is the annual Classic and Antique Cars parade. Gleaming cars (some of them dating back to the early twentieth century) that have been maintained and polished to museum standards are pulled out of storage for this occasion. Decorated with lavish daffodil and floral arrangements worthy of England's annual Chelsea Flower Show, the cars make their way along Main Street and through the heart of downtown. Crowds cheer the drivers as they head toward the eastern end of the island for the culmination of the Daffodil Festival: tailgate picnics at 'Sconset, an idyllic village of weathered shingle cottages set above a long sweep of beach and bluffs.

Tailgate picnics on Nantucket capture the islanders' collective joy at spring's arrival, where the season is welcomed as it should be: spreads call for champagne (kept chilled in ice buckets), tins and boxes and hampers of items like caviar, cold lobster, Cobb salad, rustic bread, artisan cheeses, layered cakes, and thermoses of tea.

We love any opportunity for alfresco dining. For your own spring-time tailgate picnic, we've put together a menu that can (mostly) be eaten without utensils and that satisfies an appetite built by a day spent outside in the fresh spring air. These recipes can be prepared in advance and transported to your picnic in a sturdy basket. Other than spoons and large mugs for the chowder, and forks for the potato salad, you'll just need plates, lots of napkins, and glassware for the wine. Set up your camp, raise a glass, and dig in!

NANTUCKET CLAM CHOWDER

This recipe looks like quite a few steps, but the chowder comes together quite easily. I also find that using the potato flour or potato starch, in place of flour, creates a beautiful smoothness to the broth and reinforces the flavor of the potatoes.

You may notice that I have omitted the salt in this recipe. The clams seem to contribute all the salt needed. Use any size clam you like. Littlenecks are the most readily available at the fish markets here but if you are digging your own clams for this chowder, the bigger the better! Serve this chowder with oyster crackers (see the recipe on page 47).

INGREDIENTS

4 dozen live littleneck clams, scrubbed

1 (750-ml) bottle white wine (anything crisp, like a Muscadet or Picpoul)

8 bay leaves

4 sprigs fresh thyme plus 1 tablespoon whole fresh thyme leaves

Clam juice, as needed

½ cup (1 stick) unsalted butter

2 white onions, diced

6 celery stalks, diced

3 pounds Yukon Gold or russet potatoes (peeled or unpeeled—your choice),
    cut into ½-inch dice

¼ cup potato flour or potato starch

2 teaspoons freshly ground black pepper

4 cups heavy cream

Place the clams in a large stockpot with the wine, 4 bay leaves, and the 4 whole sprigs of thyme; set over high heat and cover with a tight-fitting lid to keep the steam in the pot. Reduce the heat to medium. As soon as all the clams have opened (the cooking time will vary depending on the size of the clams, but it should take 2 to 5 minutes), remove the pot from the heat and set aside until the clams are cool enough to handle.

(continued)

Using tongs, remove the clams from the pot, being sure to let any liquid stay in the pot, and transfer them to a bowl. Using a small sharp knife, remove the clam meat from the shells and set aside. Dispose of the shells but keep any liquid that accumulates in the bowl and add it to the broth in the stockpot.

Strain the clam broth by pouring it through a fine-mesh sieve lined with a few layers of cheesecloth (or a clean linen kitchen towel) set over a large bowl; you should have 5 cups of broth; if not, add clam juice to reach this amount. Coarsely chop the clam meat, add it to the strained broth, and set aside.

Rinse and dry the stockpot, set it over medium heat, and add the butter. Once the butter has melted, add the onions and celery. Cook, stirring occasionally with a wooden spoon, until the onions are slightly translucent but not browned. Add the potatoes, potato flour, pepper, remaining 4 bay leaves, and thyme leaves and stir to combine. Add the cream and cook over low heat, stirring frequently to ensure the cream does not become scorched, until the potatoes are tender.

Return the strained broth and chopped clam meat to the stockpot. Stir gently and simmer over low heat for another 10 minutes or until thoroughly heated. Serve immediately.

THE CHARM OF 'SCONSET

How is it that an island only fourteen miles across at its widest and five in the other direction can have such a range of scenery? Miles and miles of sandy beaches, rose-covered dunes, moors that seem to stretch to the horizon, cranberry bogs, undulating hills, harbors and creeks, bluffs and cliffs, woods and fields—all comprise the spectacular topography of Nantucket.

The architecture on the island is just as striking and diverse. Downtown, you'll find stately brick, granite, and clapboard Georgian buildings, cobblestone paving, iron streetlamps, and brick sidewalks. A few miles away, on the eastern end of the island, it's a different world.

There, you'll find Siasconset, a long-settled village (since 1670) that goes by a number of names and spellings—'Sconset, Sconset, Seconset, depending on the source. But on the island, 'Sconset is how it's pronounced and spelled. The name's origin is Wampanoag (one of the native American tribes living on the island long before the English arrived), as is the word "Nantucket" and many of the other place names on the island.

The first European settlement at 'Sconset was a fishing village. Codfish (so plentiful in these waters), in the form of salt cod was a valuable commodity in Europe. Outposts in the then-colonies that fished for cod—and filleted, salted, and air-dried it—thrived. By the nineteenth century, 'Sconset was home to a whaling station, a business that brought great wealth to the island. A surprising number of buildings from those eras still remain and some of what constitutes modern-day 'Sconset can be recognized in the terrific collection of old black-and-white photos at the Nantucket Historical Association.

For residents and visitors today, the attraction of this end of Nantucket is its natural beauty, its quiet separateness, and its charming neighborhoods. Street after street of cedar-shingled houses weathered to a pale silver are covered with rambling roses in late spring and early summer. The roses climb over picket fences, entries, and weathered shake roofs, almost too profuse to look real.

Sankaty Head Lighthouse is here, on the bluffs that mark the easternmost point of the island. Dropping fifty feet and more to pristine powdery white sand beaches, the dramatic beauty of the bluffs is another iconic Nantucket image. But 'Sconset's most stunning feature is its wide-openness to sea and sky, and its quiet. The brilliant light, the long views, the sound of the sea—no wonder an eighteenth-century visitor described 'Sconset as the best place "to cherish contemplative ideas." We couldn't agree more.

LOBSTER ROLLS

Everyone needs to have a lobster roll when they visit Nantucket and I think ours is a beautiful representation of this New England classic: a warm, buttery toasted roll filled with super fresh lobster that we toss with lemon-spiked mayonnaise and fresh herbs. Please feel free to substitute precooked lobster meat for this recipe. Many fishmongers sell it. Our homemade rolls really do this iconic dish justice, but if baking isn't your thing, you can use store-bought split-top hot dog buns, sliced brioche, or challah bread. Whatever your choice, be sure to butter and lightly toast the bread.

INGREDIENTS

4 (1½-pound) live lobsters
½ cup mayonnaise
2 lemons, zested and juiced
8 Homemade Rolls (recipe follows)
Butter, softened

2 tablespoons coarsely chopped celery leaves
  (light green only)
1 tablespoon chopped fresh tarragon leaves
  (lightly chopped right before using)
1 tablespoon chopped fresh chives

Fill two large stockpots halfway with water and bring them to a boil over high heat. Once the water is rapidly boiling, add 2 lobsters to each pot, turn off the heat, and cover the pots with their lids. After 30 minutes, drain the lobsters and let them cool completely on a baking sheet.

Split the lobster tail down the back using a pair of kitchen scissors; remove and discard the intestine. Using the kitchen scissors again, remove the meat from the lobster knuckles. Cover each claw with a clean kitchen towel and crack them with the *back* of a chef's knife. After removing all the meat from the shells, check it carefully for pieces of shell. Cut the meat into bite-size pieces.

(continued)

In a large bowl, mix the chopped lobster meat with the mayonnaise and lemon zest and juice. Cover and chill until ready to serve (the lobster salad can be stored in the refrigerator for 1 day).

Preheat a griddle or large (12-inch) skillet over medium heat. Make a 1-inch-deep slice in the tops of the rolls. Butter the sides of each roll and toast them lightly until golden on all sides. Watch closely so they don't burn.

Divide the lobster salad among the toasted rolls and garnish with the chopped fresh herbs.

HOMEMADE ROLLS

This recipe makes ten rolls, which means you'll have two extras to eat fresh out of the oven with butter.

4 teaspoons active dry yeast
1½ cups water, room temperature
3¼ cups all-purpose flour
¼ cup sugar
¼ cup vegetable oil or olive oil
1½ teaspoons kosher salt
1 egg beaten with 1 tablespoon water

In a large bowl, dissolve the yeast in the water. Add the flour, sugar, oil, and salt and combine with a rubber spatula. Once the dough comes together, turn it out onto a well-floured countertop and knead for a few minutes until the dough is smooth. Place the dough in a clean and lightly oiled bowl; cover with a clean kitchen towel and let the dough rise for 45 minutes or until doubled in size.

Turn the dough out onto the countertop again, this time with only a light dusting of flour. Divide the dough in half and then each half into 5 portions. Roll each portion of dough into a 5-inch log. Place the logs on a baking sheet that has been rubbed with oil and lightly dusted with flour, side by side and barely touching. Cover the baking sheet with a clean kitchen towel and let the rolls rise for 25 to 30 minutes.

Preheat the oven to 400°F. With a pastry brush, paint the rolls lightly with the egg wash, being careful not to deflate the rolls. Bake the rolls for 12 to 15 minutes or until the tops are evenly golden brown. Transfer to a wire rack to cool completely.

Located on the French Riviera in Provençe, the winery has built its reputation on innovation, style, and quality. Three rosé wines from this house are on the menu at CRU; for the tailgate picnic recipes in this chapter, we recommend the **Château Romassan.**

This Bandol rosé is rich in character thanks to Mourvédre, the predominant grape in the blend. Its pale, ethereal pink color is tinged with gold, and in the glass it releases a bouquet of citrus fruits. Grown in exceptionally dry, sunny weather in a soil comprised of limestone, sandstone, and sandy marl, **Château Romassan**'s taste is lively and bright, with notes of pink grapefruit, the fruity roundness of Syrah, and a finish that is complex and lasting.

A LOVELY WHITE WINE FOR SPRING ALFRESCO DINING

For a white wine, we love Alex Gambal's **Saint Aubin Mergers des Dent des Chien.** Produced in Burgundy, home of his winery Maison Alex Gambal, this premier cru was one of the first wines he created for the domaine. A beautiful pale gold, this wine showcases an elegant nose with notes of ripe lemon and toasted brioche. A perfect match with our lobster roll.

Domaines Ott produces friendly and elegant handcrafted wines. We love them as a progression with any meal. Pale and pretty, these wines are a crystal-clear pink with orange or gold undertones.

OYSTER CRACKERS WITH CRACKED FENNEL SEEDS

We knew we were going to be selling a lot of clam chowder at CRU, but I hated the thought of giving our guests oyster crackers in small plastic bags. I loved the idea of serving little biscuits alongside the chowder but they would need to be crispy, with the texture of a cracker. This recipe hits the mark. It starts like biscuit dough but uses much less liquid. We even repeatedly stack the dough as it is being rolled out to create flaky, biscuit-like layers. An added plus: the dough may be rolled into sheets and frozen until ready to use.

INGREDIENTS

1½ teaspoons fennel seeds
2 cups all-purpose flour
2 teaspoons kosher salt
1 teaspoon baking powder

½ cup (1 stick) unsalted butter,
    cut into small cubes and chilled, plus
    2 tablespoons melted
½ cup whole milk

Preheat the oven to 375°F.

Lightly crush the fennel seeds in a mortar and pestle. Combine the flour, salt, and baking powder in a large bowl; stir in the crushed fennel seeds.

Work the chilled butter into the dry ingredients with your fingers, until the butter is pea-sized. Add the milk and melted butter to the dough. Gently mix until it forms a ball.

On a lightly floured surface, cut the dough in half and stack one half on top of the other. Roll it out to a 6-inch square; repeat the cutting, stacking, and rolling two more times. Roll the dough out to ¼-inch thickness and square off the edges. Cut the dough into 1-by-1-inch squares and place on parchment-lined baking sheets about 1 inch apart. Refrigerate for 30 minutes.

Bake for 20 minutes or until light golden brown. Transfer to a wire rack and let cool completely before storing in an airtight container. Can be stored for a week.

NOTE: A glass or ceramic container will keep the crackers crisper than plastic.

SPICED FRIED CHICKEN

This chicken is an ode to my days at Oleana restaurant in Cambridge. Ana Sortun would marinate her chicken with a heavy hand of sweet Turkish spices before frying. I now make this recipe for our annual Daffodil Days picnic, and often throughout the summer. It never lasts very long.

When I make this recipe at home, I prefer to use an outdoor deep-fryer, the kind many people use for a turkey. The chicken cooks quickly and evenly, *and* the fried food smell stays out of the house! Use a high-heat probe thermometer periodically to check the temperature of the oil and the chicken; this step helps ensure crispy juicy chicken every time. Or use a thermostatically controlled deep-fryer (specialty kitchenware shops sell them).

The chicken needs to marinate for at least four hours, or overnight, so keep that in mind as you plan a picnic that includes this recipe.

INGREDIENTS

2 cups buttermilk

2 tablespoons sugar

2 teaspoons kosher salt

2 teaspoons freshly ground black pepper

½ teaspoon ground

½ teaspoon smoked paprika

½ teaspoon ground cumin

½ teaspoon grated nutmeg

½ teaspoon dried oregano

1 (5- to 6-pound) chicken, cut into 10 pieces, or 8 chicken thighs or other cuts of your preference

Vegetable oil for frying

1½ cups all-purpose flour

½ teaspoon iodized salt (I use iodized salt in the flour dredge as I find that kosher salt does not blend as well)

Combine the buttermilk, sugar, salt, pepper, cinnamon, paprika, cumin, nutmeg, and oregano in a large bowl or resealable plastic bag. Add the chicken pieces and refrigerate for at least 4 hours and preferably overnight.

(continued)

Fill a deep-fryer with oil and heat to 350°F.

Place the flour and salt in a shallow bowl. Dredge the chicken 2 pieces at a time in the flour, pressing so that the flour clings to the buttermilk coating on the chicken. Let the dredged chicken rest on a parchment-lined tray until the oil has come up to temperature. Fry a few pieces of chicken at a time for 8 to 10 minutes or until the internal temperature of the meat has reached at least 160°F. Using tongs, carefully remove the chicken from the oil and place on wire racks lined with brown paper or paper towels. Let rest for a minimum of 5 minutes before serving, or let cool completely before packing for a picnic.

NOTE: To keep the coating as crisp as possible, after the 5-minute rest period, transfer the chicken to unlined wire racks.

POTATO SALAD WITH CAPERS AND SOFT-COOKED EGGS

→ SERVES 6 TO 8 ←

I love a French-style potato salad with ingredients like punchy Dijon mustard and shallots with vinegar and tarragon. But I miss the sweet creaminess of the American version with its pickle relish and mayonnaise. This recipe combines the best of both worlds. It is creamy, tangy, and slightly sweet—the perfect addition to a fried chicken picnic.

INGREDIENTS

3½ pounds Red Bliss or other thin-skinned potatoes,
  unpeeled, quartered if they are small, or cut into
  six pieces if they are larger
2 tablespoons kosher salt
4 extra large eggs
4 shallots, thinly sliced
¼ cup white wine vinegar
1 tablespoon sugar
1½ cups mayonnaise
¼ cup Dijon mustard
¼ cup capers, drained
3 tablespoons fresh lemon juice (1 lemon)
2 tablespoons coarsely chopped fresh dill, plus extra for garnish
2 tablespoons coarsely chopped fresh tarragon, plus extra for garnish
½ teaspoon freshly ground black pepper

Add the potatoes to a large stockpot and cover with water and kosher salt. Place over high heat and bring to a boil; immediately reduce the heat to a simmer and cook for 15 to 20 minutes or until the potatoes are tender. Drain the potatoes and set aside.

(continued)

Bring a small pot of water to a boil. Gently lower the eggs into the water and cook for 7 minutes. Immediately cool the eggs under cold running water. Once cool enough to handle, peel and slice the eggs in half. (The yolks will be golden, soft, and custardy, not hard and pale yellow.)

In a large mixing bowl, combine the shallots, vinegar, and sugar. Let sit for 5 minutes. Add the mayonnaise, mustard, capers, lemon juice, dill, tarragon, pepper, and cooked potatoes. Stir gently with a wooden spoon to combine. Garnish the salad with the eggs and sprinkle with additional tarragon and dill. Serve at room temperature or refrigerate until ready to serve.

BITTERSWEET CHOCOLATE WHOOPIE PIES WITH SEA-SALT BUTTERCREAM

» MAKES 36 WHOOPIE PIES «

If your experience with whoopie pies has been limited to the kind sold in supermarkets, encased in a plastic wrapper with an expiration date stamped on the back, you're in for a treat. These desserts are delicious, and perfect for a picnic since no utensils are required. The filling here is rich with vanilla (and the surprisingly perfect addition of flake sea salt), and the cake-like cookies that surround it are intensely chocolate.

This recipe makes a big batch but the "pies" freeze well. Having a dozen or so in the freezer means you're ready with a special treat when the mood strikes.

FOR THE CAKES

⅓ cup bittersweet chocolate, chopped

¾ cup hot coffee

2½ cups all-purpose flour

1 cup cocoa powder

1 tablespoon baking powder

½ tablespoon kosher salt

1 cup (2 sticks) unsalted butter, softened

2 cups sugar

2 extra large eggs

1 tablespoon vanilla extract

1⅔ cups buttermilk

FOR THE SEA-SALT BUTTERCREAM

1 pound (4 sticks) unsalted butter, softened

1 cup marshmallow creme

3 cups confectioners' sugar

2 tablespoons vanilla paste

2 teaspoons flake sea salt, such as
Maldon salt

TO MAKE THE CAKES: Preheat the oven to 400°F.

Place the chocolate in a small bowl and pour the hot coffee over it. Stir gently with a fork as the chocolate melts; set aside and let cool to room temperature.

Combine the flour, cocoa, baking powder, and salt and set aside.

(continued)

Using a mixer with the paddle attachment, beat the butter and sugar until very light and fluffy. Add the eggs one at a time and then the vanilla extract, beating until very light and airy. Add the chocolate-coffee mixture; combine thoroughly.

Add half of the flour mixture and half of the buttermilk; mix until well incorporated. Repeat with the remaining dry ingredients and buttermilk.

Line 2 baking sheets with parchment paper. Fill a piping bag fitted with a $\frac{1}{2}$-inch round tip (or a 1-gallon sealable storage bag with a $\frac{1}{2}$-inch hole cut in one corner) with one-third of the whoopie pie batter. Pipe 2-inch-wide circles, 1 inch tall, leaving at least 2 inches between them. (A standard-size baking sheet should hold a dozen per tray, three across and four down.)

Bake for 5 to 8 minutes, or until the cakes are just set. Transfer the sheets to a wire rack and let cool completely before removing the cakes with a spatula. Set the cakes aside and repeat piping and baking until all the batter has been used; you should end up with about 72 cakes, which will give you 36 filled whoopie pies.

TO MAKE THE SEA-SALT BUTTERCREAM: Using a mixer with the paddle attachment, beat the butter until light and fluffy. Add the marshmallow creme and beat again to combine. Slowly add the sugar, vanilla paste, and salt and combine thoroughly, then beat on high speed for 5 minutes.

Place one-third of the buttercream in a piping bag fitted with a $\frac{1}{2}$-inch round tip (or a 1-gallon sealable storage bag with a $\frac{1}{2}$-inch hole cut in one corner). Hold a cake flat side up and, starting in the center of it, pipe 1 to 2 tablespoons of buttercream filling over it evenly. Top gently with another cake; set aside and continue until all the cakes are filled, refilling the piping bag as you go. Serve.

NOTE: The whoopie pies may be stored at room temperature unless it is very warm, in which case they should be refrigerated. They may also be placed on parchment-lined baking sheets, wrapped tightly in plastic wrap, and frozen. Thaw at room temperature.

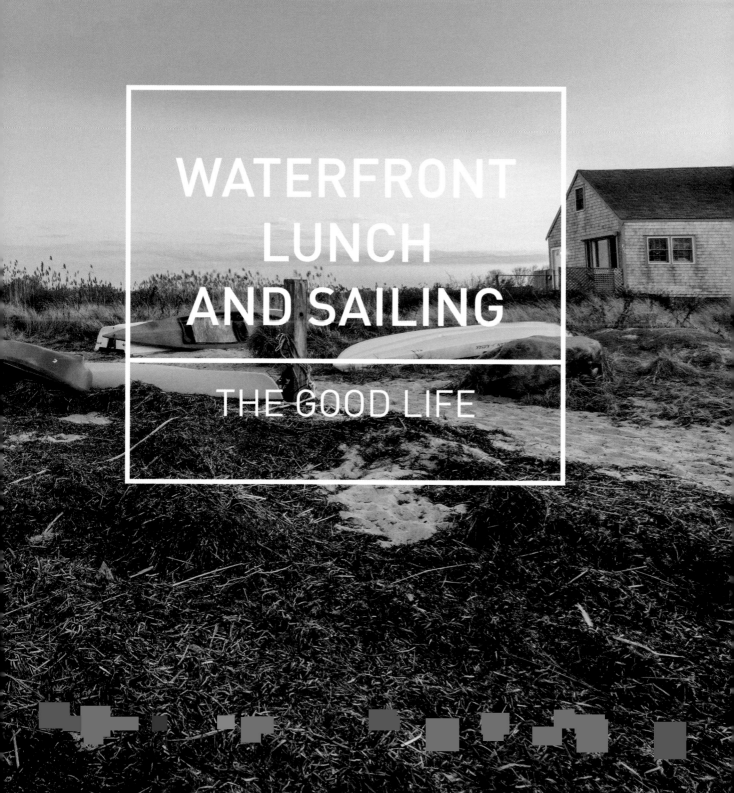

WATERFRONT
LUNCH
AND SAILING

THE GOOD LIFE

Every spring, as the weather warms, the island begins to hum. Farm stands come to life with vibrant color, hotels bustle with guests arriving from around the world, and hundreds of sail and motor yachts come and go from their moorings in the harbor. The roses are coming into bloom: fragrant *Rosa rugosa* grow wild along the beach roads and dunes, and it seems a picture-postcard variety of climbing, rambling, and shrub roses are cultivated in every yard. The storefronts downtown beckon with gorgeous clothing, jewelry, home décor items, and more—much of it unique to these shops—offering a world-class experience for the sophisticated shopper.

Adding to the excitement is an annual three-day weekend of sailboat racing at the end of May that kicks off the summer season on Nantucket. It's called the Figawi Race Weekend, known internationally as a premier sail-racing event. More than two hundred sailboats and their crews participate, while thousands of avid sailors and spectators from the United States, Europe, and the Caribbean arrive to celebrate the sport.

The sailors head out from Hyannis, on Cape Cod, racing around courses across Nantucket Sound and finishing at the entrance to Nantucket Harbor. From late morning until early afternoon, the waters off Brant Point sparkle with sleek hulls and massive sails, moving fast and impossibly close. The race ends with a colorful, friendly, champagne-popping parade of the boats into Nantucket Boat Basin.

CRU's chic dining rooms, back bar, and waterfront lounge are *the* place to take in the action over lunch with friends after a morning of shopping in the trendy boutiques downtown. As colorful racing flags snap in the breeze and the boats make their way into the harbor, our guests raise a toast. No matter who won the race, wine flows and Nantucket's esprit de corps rules the day.

The recipes selected for this chapter showcase the best of the season on Nantucket. In late spring, the waters around the island are still cold but have warmed up enough for the oysters to grow plump and full of flavor; lobsters are sweet and tender; and local fishermen are bringing in fresh fluke and black bass daily. The farmers' markets are bursting with early produce, particularly radishes in a rainbow of colors. And that brief but magical season when the native strawberries are ripe is just beginning.

With the sublime recipes in this chapter and a good bottle of Chablis, you can revisit the first race weekend of the season and your waterfront lunch at CRU with friends. The scents from your kitchen will transport you to that late-spring day when you basked in the sunshine, sipping a perfectly chilled wine as gorgeous boats glided into Nantucket Harbor, their decks filled with cheering crews.

CRISPY FRIED OYSTERS WITH BIBB LETTUCE AND RADISH RÉMOULADE

→ SERVES 4 ←

I have always loved celery root rémoulade but during spring I substitute radishes for the celery root and this version is fantastic with fried oysters. To serve, we set a fried oyster in a leaf of Bibb lettuce, and top it with a bit of the rémoulade, fresh herbs, and a healthy squeeze of fresh lemon juice. The little packages are meant to be picked up and eaten out of hand, which our guests love! As it sits, the rémoulade will turn a very pale pink from the radishes—so pretty for spring.

FOR THE RADISH RÉMOULADE

1 bunch red radishes (10–12 ounces), trimmed (a mixture of any type of radishes, including watermelon, lime, black, and daikon is fine)
½ cup mayonnaise
2 tablespoons capers
1 tablespoon sliced cornichons
1 tablespoon fresh lemon juice
1½ teaspoons Dijon mustard

FOR THE OYSTERS

24 medium-to-large oysters, shucked
¾ cup all-purpose flour
Kosher salt and freshly ground black pepper
2 extra large eggs
¼ cup buttermilk
2 cups panko breadcrumbs
Vegetable oil for frying (about 1½ cups)
1 head Bibb lettuce (also known as Boston or butter lettuce), leaves separated
1 tablespoon chopped fresh chives
1 tablespoon fresh tarragon or chervil leaves
1 lemon, cut in 4 wedges

(continued)

TO MAKE THE RÉMOULADE: Julienne the radishes as thinly as possible and gently mix with the mayonnaise, capers, cornichons, lemon juice, and mustard. Place in a glass jar with a tight-fitting lid and refrigerate until needed.

TO PREPARE THE OYSTERS: Place the flour in a shallow bowl and add a pinch each of salt and pepper; beat the eggs in a second bowl and stir in the buttermilk; and place the panko in a third bowl. Working with two or three at a time, dredge the oysters in the flour mixture, then dip in the buttermilk and, finally into the panko, pressing lightly to make sure a good coating of panko sticks to the oysters. Set the breaded oysters on a parchment-lined baking sheet and refrigerate until you are ready to fry them. (The oysters may be breaded up to 4 hours in advance.)

Add enough oil to a wide, deep-sided cast-iron Dutch oven or skillet to reach a depth of about 1 inch and heat over medium to medium-high heat until it shimmers. Place the breaded oysters in the hot oil and fry until they begin browning around the edges; turn them and continue frying until golden brown on both sides. Remove with a slotted spoon, set on a baking sheet lined with brown paper or paper towels, and sprinkle with a little salt.

TO ASSEMBLE: Arrange the lettuce leaves on a platter. Top each leaf with a fried oyster and a dollop of rémoulade. Sprinkle with the chives and tarragon and serve immediately with lemon wedges.

Mark Valeriani, lead brewer at Cisco Brewers, in collaboration with the winemaker at Nantucket Vineyards and the distiller at Triple Eight Distillery, directs and oversees production of Fifth Bend Oyster Stout. The brewing coincides with the arrival of spring and Nantucket's Daffodil Festival. Every year Cisco and CRU coordinate with Simon Edwards at Fifth Bend Oysters for the annual delivery of oysters to begin the brewing process.

In a blind tasting, you won't necessarily identify this brew as a stout. Lighter and easy to drink for a dark beer in the warm weather, it almost comes across as a dark brown ale with smoked malt tones, coffee notes, and hints of brine. Its soft bitterness, low on hops and bright on minerals, make this oyster stout a good pairing with CRU's fried oysters and pork belly or Chef Erin's mussels with chorizo.

The refreshing and full-flavored effervescence of beer is a great choice for a late-spring or early-summer lunch, particularly enjoyed out of doors. Here are three of our top picks:

TRUTH AMERICAN IPA, RHINEGEIST BREWERY, OHIO, USA. ABV 7.20%

This beer is a modern IPA brewed with a nod to the Pacific, tasted in its hop backbone and hint of tropical fruits. Its mango and grapefruit notes provide a soft bitterness that pairs well with oysters. Amarillo, Simcoe, Citra, and Centennial hops are some of the most tropical and citrusy while maintaining a dry finish, complementing the brisk salt air of Nantucket and the brininess of our local oysters.

CRU'S FIFTH BEND OYSTER STOUT, CISCO BREWERS, NANTUCKET, MA, USA. ABV 5.10%

This stout is made exclusively for CRU and uses local Fifth Bend oysters and their shells.

JULIUS ECHTER HEFE-WEISSBIER HELL, WURZBURG HOFBRAU, GERMANY. ABV 5.30%

This Hefeweizen comes from one of Germany's oldest breweries. It's a cloudy, auburn-colored beer with a full creamy head. Brewed with a mix of 70 percent wheat and 30 percent barley, it also contains a small sediment of yeast that produces a secondary fermentation. Fans enjoy its smooth, creamy texture with barely noticeable hops. We like its medium- to full-bodied characteristics and its flavors of banana nut bread, clove, and nutmeg. A slightly earthy lemon meringue finish makes it a perfect seafood pairing.

LOBSTER SALAD WITH GRAPEFRUIT, AVOCADO, AND QUINOA

This is an early-summer version of one of our most popular lunch staples at CRU: lobster salad. During the height of the summer we substitute crunchy farm-fresh cucumbers and radishes for the avocado and grapefruit in this beautiful and healthful salad.

INGREDIENTS

2 tablespoons lemon zest, 6 tablespoons lemon juice

1 teaspoon honey

1 teaspoon Dijon mustard

½ teaspoon kosher salt

¾ cup extra-virgin olive oil

1 pound cooked, picked, and cleaned lobster meat (see page 43)

4 cups mixed baby greens, watercress, or arugula

1 large avocado, peeled, pitted, and sliced

1 ruby-red grapefruit, peeled and segmented

1 bunch fresh mint leaves, torn into small pieces

1 cup cooked golden quinoa, chilled

½ cup sliced almonds, toasted

Sea salt and freshly ground black pepper

In a bowl, whisk together the lemon zest, juice, honey, Dijon and salt. Slowly add the oil. Place the lobster meat, greens, avocado, grapefruit, mint, quinoa, and almonds in a large bowl and toss gently. Drizzle the lemon dressing over the mixture and toss gently again. Season with salt and pepper to taste. Divide among individual salad plates and serve immediately.

BLACK BASS CRUDO WITH GREEN TOMATO AND LEMON VERBENA SALSA

→ SERVES 4 ←

I met my friend Kevin while we were working together on the northern coast of France. Years later, Kevin came to help me out one busy summer weekend in Nantucket. We came up with this recipe after visiting a few of the local farms together. This salsa is terrific on countless dishes, including raw or grilled fish and oysters. We even top slices of fresh mozzarella with it. It is summer freshness by the spoonful.

The recipe can be made with unripe green tomatoes in the early summer and then a month or so later with gorgeous, juicy green zebra tomatoes.

FOR THE SALSA

1 cup lemon verbena leaves
½ cup light olive oil or vegetable oil
1 large green tomato, cored and finely chopped
1 shallot, finely chopped
½ green jalapeño, finely chopped
1½ tablespoons fresh lemon juice
½ teaspoon kosher salt

FOR THE CRUDO

1½ pounds black bass fillets, skin and bones removed
2 lemon verbena leaves, finely sliced
Flake sea salt

TO MAKE THE SALSA: Puree 1 cup lemon verbena leaves with the oil in a blender until very smooth. Strain the oil through a fine-mesh sieve. (The oil can be made up to 2 days ahead of time and refrigerated until ready to use; it can also be frozen.)

Combine the tomato, shallot, jalapeño, lemon juice, and salt in a small bowl and stir in 2 teaspoons of the verbena oil. Reserve the remaining oil for the crudo.

TO MAKE THE CRUDO: Thinly slice the bass and arrange the pieces on a chilled plate. Top the bass with the green tomato salsa and drizzle additional verbena oil over the top. Sprinkle with the sliced lemon verbena leaves and flake sea salt and serve immediately.

NOTE: If lemon verbena is unavailable, you can use lemon balm or fresh mint in its place.

FLUKE MEUNIÈRE

The first time I tasted sole meunière—a classic French dish—I was in the small fishing port of Concarneau, in the northwest of France. It was so simple, so perfect. When we started planning for CRU, I knew that was *exactly* how I wanted to serve the local Nantucket fluke. As an accompaniment to the fish, I developed a new take on a childhood favorite of mine, green beans amandine. I don't know if this signature CRU dish will ever change but I hope not.

INGREDIENTS

4 tablespoons (½ stick) unsalted butter

½ cinnamon stick

6 fresh sage leaves

4 half-pound fluke fillets

Kosher salt

1 tablespoon fine flour, such as Wondra

2 tablespoons vegetable oil

1 pound haricots vert or green beans, blanched

1½ tablespoons fresh lemon juice, plus 1 lemon, cut into 4 wedges

½ cup hazelnuts, skins removed, toasted and lightly crushed

In a small saucepan, melt the butter with the cinnamon stick. Set a fine-mesh sieve over a bowl with tall sides. Place the sage leaves in the bowl beneath the sieve. When the butter smells like caramel and is the color of toasted hazelnuts, remove the pan from the heat and pour the butter slowly and carefully through the sieve; the sage leaves will flavor the butter and the heat of the butter will "crisp" the sage.

TO COOK THE FISH: Season the fish fillets with salt and then dust them with the flour. Heat the oil in a 14-inch skillet over medium-high heat. When the pan is very hot but not smoking, gently place the fillets, flesh side down, in the pan. Give the fish a little shake to ensure that it isn't sticking, then lower the heat to medium. Cook until the flesh turns golden; carefully flip and cook another minute or two. If you do not have a pan

(continued)

that's large enough to cook all the fillets at once, use two pans or place the first batch of cooked fish on a baking sheet in a warm oven (200°F). Wipe out the pan and repeat the cooking process with the last two fillets.

FINISHING THE GREEN BEANS: As soon as you flip the last fillet, transfer the butter and the crispy sage leaves to a large sauté pan over medium heat, add the blanched green beans, and toss. Add the lemon juice and toasted hazelnuts, toss, and remove from the heat.

TO SERVE: Divide the beans among four plates. Top each with a fillet of fish. Garnish with the lemon wedges and serve immediately.

On a clear summer day, Nantucket Sound—the sizeable body of water that lies between the southern coast of Cape Cod and Nantucket Island, bounded by Martha's Vineyard to the west and the Atlantic Ocean to the east—can appear to be nothing more than a pretty thirty- by fifty-mile stretch of open water. And indeed, it is pretty. But beneath its sapphire-blue surface lie hazards. Shallows and shoals abound. Anyone other than skilled sailors and top-notch navigators attempting to traverse this body of water risks running aground.

Its location also lends the drama of strong currents that can catch a novice (and even veteran sailors) off guard. The Sound's wide eastern end meets the ocean, which means fog is not uncommon; unpredictable winds and high seas can wreak havoc as well. In the Island's early history (pre-GPS and the other sophisticated navigation tools that are available today), shipwrecks in these waters were common.

The Sound is heavily transited: research vessels from Woods Hole; merchant ships; US Coast Guard boats; commercial fishing vessels from Fairhaven, New Bedford, and ports farther west as well as Hyannis, Martha's Vineyard, and Nantucket; sport fishing boats; pleasure boats; and ferries. It all makes for what some sailors describe as a "circus of boats"—fun to look at but also a potential danger, particularly to sail racers.

These challenges only make Nantucket Sound more appealing to sailing enthusiasts. The annual Figawi Race, from Hyannis to Nantucket and, three days later, back again, is a tradition among expert sailors from as far away as Europe and the Caribbean. The Opera House Cup Regatta is a cherished sailing tradition held the third Sunday of August with all wooden, single-hulled classic boats.

Still, the waters of the Sound are inviting, and the reward of docking at the end of the day on Nantucket—one of the world's most beautiful islands—makes the lure irresistible.

KEY LIME PIE JARS WITH A COCONUT GRAHAM CRACKER CRUST

→ SERVES 8 ←

It was no surprise when Carlos, originally from Miami, requested a Key lime pie on the CRU menu (in addition to lobster 164 different ways . . .). Slicing and serving perfect pieces of a delicate pie in a busy restaurant was my only concern. That's when the jam jars came to the rescue. These single-serve pies are as easy as they are delicious, and everyone loves them. The jars are also perfect for picnics or an afternoon at the beach. When I make this pie at home, however, I bake it in a 12-inch tart pan.

FOR THE PIE FILLING

2 (14-ounce) cans sweetened condensed milk
1½ cups Key lime juice
8 egg yolks

FOR THE CRUST

¾ cup (1½ sticks) unsalted butter
2 cups graham cracker crumbs
1 cup unsweetened shredded coconut, toasted
½ teaspoon kosher salt

FOR THE WHIPPED CREAM

2 cups heavy cream
2 teaspoons confectioners' sugar
2 teaspoons grated lime zest

Preheat the oven to 350°F.

TO MAKE THE FILLING: Whisk the condensed milk, lime juice, and egg yolks together. Set aside.

TO MAKE THE CRUST: In a medium saucepan, cook the butter over medium heat until it begins to brown and smells like caramel. Remove from the heat and add the graham cracker crumbs, toasted coconut, and salt; mix together well.

Set eight 8-ounce canning jars on a baking sheet. Spoon 2 tablespoons of the crust mixture into each jar; do not pack down. Bake for 5 minutes, then remove the jars. Divide the filling among the jars and bake for 12 to 15 minutes or until the center of the filling is just set. Transfer to a wire rack and let cool completely.

TO WHIP THE CREAM: Using a mixer with the whisk attachment, whip the heavy cream with the sugar until soft peaks form. Top the cooled pie jars with the whipped cream and lime zest. Serve immediately.

NOTE: To make one large tart instead of individual pies, press the crust mixture evenly into a 12-inch tart pan. Bake for 5 minutes. Add the filling and bake for 25 to 30 minutes or until the center of the tart barely moves when shaken. Transfer to a wire rack and let cool completely. Top with the whipped cream and lime zest and serve.

STRAWBERRY SHORTCAKES

While strawberry season in Nantucket is brief, when it's here the berries are amazing—small, sweet, and intensely flavored—so we put shortcake on the menu every night while we can get these beauties. It isn't fancy, but I think this nostalgic dessert is still one that everyone loves. I like to be playful with the syrup that the strawberries are tossed in, which changes based on what the farms have—lavender, angelica, and fresh chamomile are favorites. Lavender, however, gets quite a bit of play as it grows rampant at my house.

FOR THE SHORTCAKES

2 tablespoons turbinado sugar

2 cups all-purpose flour

1 tablespoon granulated sugar

1 tablespoon baking powder

1 teaspoon salt

½ cup (1 stick) unsalted butter, cut into small cubes

1 cup buttermilk

2 tablespoons heavy cream

FOR THE WHIPPED CRÈME FRAÎCHE

1 cup heavy cream

½ cup crème fraîche

2 tablespoons confectioners' sugar

1 cup Lavender Syrup (recipe follows)

2 pints strawberries, hulled and sliced

Fresh lavender flowers (optional)

TO MAKE THE SHORTCAKES: Preheat the oven to 425°F. Line a baking sheet with parchment paper and sprinkle with 1 tablespoon of turbinado sugar.

Mix the flour, granulated sugar, baking powder, and salt together in a large bowl. Add the butter and with a pastry cutter or your hands, work the butter into the dry ingredients until it has the texture of coarse cornmeal with some pea-sized bits. Stir in the buttermilk. Once combined, place the dough on a floured surface; flatten it with floured hands to a 6-by-9-inch rectangle to a generous 1-inch thickness and, using a chef's knife, cut into six 3-by-3-inch squares.

(continued)

Place the squares on the parchment-lined baking sheet. Brush the tops of the biscuits with the heavy cream and sprinkle with the remaining raw sugar. Bake for 10 to 15 minutes, until the tops are just beginning to turn golden in spots. Transfer to a wire rack.

TO MAKE THE WHIPPED CRÈME FRAÎCHE: Using a mixer with the whisk attachment, whip the cream, crème fraîche, and sugar until light and fluffy. Chill until ready to use.

Pour the lavender syrup over the strawberries. Let them sit for 10 minutes.

Cut the shortcakes in half horizontally, layer them with the strawberries and syrup, and top with the whipped crème fraîche. Garnish with fresh lavender flowers if desired. Serve immediately.

LAVENDER SYRUP

INGREDIENTS

1 cup sugar
1 cup water
8 sprigs fresh lavender

Combine the water, sugar, and lavender sprigs in a small saucepan and bring to a boil over high heat. Immediately reduce the heat to low and simmer the mixture for 5 minutes. Remove from the heat and let the syrup cool completely; strain the lavender out of the syrup.

NOTE: If fresh lavender is not available, you can substitute another herb (tarragon, for example), or go in another direction and use a split vanilla bean. You can also use a few strips of lemon, orange, or lime zest to flavor the syrup.

SUMMERTIME GRILLING AT HOME

SIMPLY PERFECT ALFRESCO DINING

School's out, July is here, and celebratory dinners at home that feature the best of the local catch and summer produce are the perfect way to entertain during the halcyon days of midsummer on Nantucket. We all want to stay outside as long as possible, and we do—lingering until the last traces of light have left the sky.

For this chapter, we've put together a menu for a summer alfresco dinner that highlights three seafood recipes and showcases the spectacular flavors of midsummer in the form of a lemony zucchini salad brightened with fresh mint, and an unforgettable tomato tart. And, as every host will appreciate, much of the menu can be prepared in advance, allowing you to enjoy the evening as much as your guests will. Dessert is satisfying but light; peaches at their peak of juicy flavorful ripeness take center stage against a delicate almond cake moistened with honey-spiked whipped cream.

We are big fans of local produce—here on the island, and in our travels during the off-season. That's why we recommend that wherever you live, you support your local growers by shopping at farm stands and farmers' markets. When you're here on the island for an extended summer vacation, why not discover what the farmers have to offer? Start a Nantucket tradition with your family: Two days a week, before the sun gets too high, take a bike ride to Bartlett's Farm or Moors End Farm and pick up enough vegetables, greens, herbs, and fruit for a few lunches and dinners. On your way, enjoy the scenery and the scented air. The magical beauty of a summer morning on New England's most beautiful island, riding along leisurely with the ones you love, will become an unforgettable image in your memory.

For a wine to accompany this menu, we recommend **Château de Selle Rosé**. This French wine from Domaines Ott (located on the Riviera, where the vines grow in arid limestone soil bathed in dazzling sunshine) is made from a blend of grape varieties from Côtes de Provence but mostly from Grenache, which gives it a delicate color. The wine's unique softness, with notes of citrus fruit, orchard flowers, and lemon, pairs beautifully with the dishes in this chapter: a chilled Mediterranean-style seafood salad of squid, tuna, mussels, and shrimp; grilled striped bass; and lobster tails in herbed butter.

Bon appétit!

RECIPES FOR
SUMMERTIME GRILLING
AT HOME

Chilled Seafood Salad

Heirloom Tomato Tart

Grilled Striped Bass with Cucumber
Tartar Sauce

Grilled Lobsters with Herb and Coral Butter

Zucchini Ribbon Salad with
Lemon Vinaigrette and Mint

Almond Cake with Fresh Peaches and
Honey Whipped Cream

CHILLED SEAFOOD SALAD

→→   SERVES 6   ←←

Jigging for squid on the harbor docks can make for good late-night fun. The squid season in Nantucket is generally in the summer and fall and it can be a bit sporadic. But when they're here, they are almost hard not to catch.

This recipe is an homage to the simple seafood salads popular along the Mediterranean coastline. Dressed with little more than olive oil and lemon, this salad is light and refreshing. It begs to be enjoyed with a chilled glass of wine.

INGREDIENTS

8 ounces squid, fresh or frozen, whole, body cleaned

1 pound (26 to 30 count) wild-caught shrimp

1 pound live mussels, debearded

8 ounces yellowfin tuna, cut into bite-size cubes

1 red Fresno chile or jalapeño, stemmed, seeded, and minced

1 tablespoon minced red onion or shallot

3 tablespoons extra-virgin olive oil

1½ tablespoons fresh lemon juice

¼ cup flat-leaf parsley leaves

Flake sea salt, such as Maldon

If using a whole squid, rinse the tentacles and bodies inside and out. Then slice the bodies (which are tube-shaped) into thin rings, separate the tentacles from the head (where the eyes and beak are), discarding the head, and separate the tentacles if they are large. Set aside.

Bring a large pot of water to a boil. Have an ice bath with a sieve set up next to the stove. Add the shrimp to the boiling water and cook for 1 minute. The shrimp will immediately turn

(continued)

opaque and firm up. Remove them with a slotted spoon and transfer to the ice bath to cool. Remove them from the cold water, place on a clean kitchen towel, and pat them dry.

Add the mussels to the same pot of boiling water. Cook the mussels for 2 to 3 minutes or until they all open. Transfer the mussels to a plate to cool. When they have cooled enough to handle, remove the meat from the shells, discarding any that don't open. Place the mussels in a large bowl with the cooked shrimp.

Lastly, add the sliced squid and tentacles to the boiling water. They will cook very quickly, in 1 minute. As soon as the squid turns white and firms up, lift the pieces out with a slotted spoon and place them in the ice bath to cool. Transfer to a clean kitchen towel and pat them dry.

Add the squid to the mussels and shrimp along with the diced tuna, red chile, and red onion. (This mixture can be chilled, covered tightly, for up to 4 hours before serving.)

Just before serving, add the oil, lemon juice, parsley, and a sprinkling of flake sea salt to the seafood; toss lightly and serve immediately.

HEIRLOOM TOMATO TART

This tart, or tomato pie as most people will call it, is an utterly delicious way to enjoy tomatoes at their summer peak. It's perfect as a starter or side dish; add a green salad and make it the main event of lunch or a light dinner.

Being originally from Illinois, I love a deep-dish Chicago-style pizza. I developed this crust to mimic those found in a classic Chicago pie. The base is flaky as a pie crust, with a little yeast added to lightly proof the dough. The result: a great pie dough that I use as often as I can. It's also perfect for any French-style pizza, such as a pissaladière or tarte flambé.

Making the dough, rolling and placing it in the tart pan, and freezing it will not only help you get ahead on your prep but also benefit the dough; the sides of the chilled dough won't cave in when baked.

FOR THE CRUST

½ teaspoon active dry yeast

⅔ cup water, room temperature

2 cups all-purpose flour

1 tablespoon sugar

1 teaspoon kosher salt

½ cup (1 stick) unsalted butter, cold, cut into cubes

FOR THE FILLING

4 ounces shredded mozzarella

4 ounces shredded cheddar

½ cup mayonnaise or crème fraîche

1 teaspoon Dijon mustard

4 large ripe tomatoes

Sea salt and freshly ground black pepper

1 heaping cup torn or coarsely chopped fresh basil

TO MAKE THE CRUST: In a small bowl, dissolve the yeast in the water; set aside. In a large bowl, whisk together the flour, sugar, and salt. Add the butter and, with your fingers, work the butter into the flour mixture until it is almost entirely broken into pea-sized pieces. Add the yeast mixture to the flour mixture and stir with a fork until the flour is evenly moistened. Turn the dough out onto a floured surface and knead for a minute or so until the dough comes together. Be careful not to overwork the dough, which will make it tough. Shape it into a ball, cover with a piece of plastic wrap, and let the dough rest for about 1 hour, until puffed up slightly but not quite doubled in size.

(continued)

Roll out the dough on a floured surface to a diameter of about 14 inches. Gently lift and place it into a 12-inch tart pan with removable bottom that has been sprayed with cooking oil. Tuck the dough against the sides of the pan so the edge will be thicker than the pie's base. Using a fork, prick the surface of the dough evenly in about 10 places; this step prevents the dough from rising and keeps it thin and crisp. Carefully place the dough-lined pan in the freezer for at least 30 minutes or until ready to fill and bake.

TO MAKE THE FILLING: Preheat the oven to 425°F.

In a bowl, combine the mozzarella, cheddar, mayonnaise, and mustard, set aside.

Core the tomatoes and slice them crosswise into thin slices (barely ¼ inch thick) with a sharp serrated knife. Lay the tomato slices on paper towels, sprinkle them with sea salt, and let them rest as you prepare the rest of the tart. (This step helps remove some of the moisture from the tomatoes, which will prevent the tart from being soggy.)

Bake the frozen tart dough for 10 to 12 minutes or until light golden-colored. Set on a wire rack and let cool for at least 10 minutes.

Spread the cheese mixture into the slightly cooled tart shell, top with the basil, and then the sliced tomatoes, arranging them in slightly overlapping concentric circles. Top the tomatoes with a grinding of black pepper. Bake the tart for 20 minutes. Let cool on a wire rack for at least 10 minutes. Slice into wedges and serve slightly warm or at room temperature.

OUR FAVORITE NANTUCKET FARM STANDS: MOORS END FARM AND BARTLETT'S FARM

Nantucket might be known for its sandy beaches, but the island is also blessed with good soil. That rich earth, plus a climate moderated by the Gulf Stream (which means an earlier spring and longer fall), and an exceptional amount of sunlight thanks to its exposure on the compass, creates an excellent environment for raising fruits and vegetables. Thankfully, the tradition of farming and growing crops on the island has not died out. As a matter of fact, it's thriving.

Our island farmers and growers plant and harvest an amazing variety of fruits, vegetables, herbs, and flowers. These goods can be found at farm stands around the island and at select markets. Offerings also include local honey and locally made preserves.

As islanders ourselves, and in our roles as the owners of CRU Oyster Bar Nantucket, we are delighted to have access to fresh, locally grown produce during Nantucket's long growing season. During the months that CRU is open (May through October), a lot of what we serve is raised right here on the island. We feel good about that because (1) fresh, local produce has more flavor (and nutrients), and (2) supporting local farms and growers means sustaining open space on the island. This is why we have been proud members of Sustainable Nantucket since day one.

The two farms we are especially fond of and that grow much of what is on the seasonally changing menu at CRU are Moors End Farm and Bartlett's Farm.

Moors End Farm is a family-owned and -operated business that sits on a twenty-eight-acre spread on Polpis Road. Not far from Nantucket Harbor, the location is virtually midway on the island's east-to-west stretch. The farm's genesis was as a small vegetable stand, when, in the mid-1970s, Steve and Sue Slosek decided to try selling the extra produce from their garden. That enterprise was a success. Now, Moors End Farm cultivates twenty acres and raises a rainbow of crops.

On the southwest end of the island, not far from the Atlantic Ocean, **Bartlett's Farm** is the largest and oldest farm on Nantucket. Established in 1843 and now a sixth-generation family-owned and -operated farm, Bartlett's includes 125 acres of cultivated fields, several acres of certified organic fields, and an increasing number of organic greenhouses. In addition to the freshly picked fruits and vegetables, Bartlett's Farm is home to a full-scale 18,000-square-foot grocery market that stocks a wonderful selection of specialty cheeses, baked goods, prepared foods from the farm's commercial kitchen, and pretty much anything you might need for your pantry.

Depending on the time of year, the offerings at both farms can include strawberries, asparagus, salad greens, radishes, snap peas, cucumbers, green beans, an alphabet of

herbs from basil to thyme, broccoli, beets, carrots, raspberries, tomatoes, peppers, sweet corn, summer squashes, blueberries, turnips, kale, winter squashes, and pumpkins. Oh, and a variety of beautiful cut flowers for your table. During the abundant growing season, let their vibrant displays of fruits, herbs, and vegetables of-the-day dictate your menu!

GRILLED STRIPED BASS WITH CUCUMBER TARTAR SAUCE

Grilling striped bass at a barbecue with friends is one of my first and fondest memories of living in Nantucket. After being on the water all day, to come back home, relax with some drinks, and cook with friends and family—that's perfection.

The striped bass we catch in Nantucket is typically big and meaty. It will take some time to cook. Don't rush it. Let the fish cook on one side until it will easily lift off the grill and then repeat on the other side.

INGREDIENTS

6 striped bass fillets, 6 to 8 ounces each
¼ cup Striped Bass Marinade (recipe follows)
Kosher salt
Vegetable oil
Cucumber Tartar Sauce (page 95)

Preheat the grill to medium-high heat. If the fish still has its skin, make sure the skin has been scaled and then with a very sharp knife, score the skin without slicing into the flesh. Coat the flesh of the fish with the marinade and let the fish rest at room temperature while the grill is heating up.

Season each side of the fish with salt. Quickly wipe the grill with a little oil. Cook the fish skin side down for 6 to 8 minutes or until the fish will release from the grill. Carefully flip the fish and cook for another 5 minutes on the other side or until the flesh can be gently pulled apart.

Serve with the cucumber tartar sauce.

STRIPED BASS MARINADE

» MAKES 1 CUP «

This is the marinade we have been making at CRU since we opened. It is based on a classic Moroccan chermoula, which is typically used to flavor fish dishes. My first experience with chermoula was in the city of Essaouira on the Moroccan coast. Jane and I would visit the fishing port in Essaouira each day for lunch. We would walk through the rows of fish stalls and pick out the fish we wanted. The fishmonger would butcher the fish and liberally coat it with a vibrant marinade of cilantro, parsley, garlic, lemon, and spices. The fish could then be grilled or fried.

During the summer at CRU we will toss fresh squid in the marinade before it hits the grill and the fluke for our crispy fish sandwich gets a quick dip in this delicious mixture before it gets battered and fried. Try it on any seafood you will be grilling, roasting, or sautéing.

INGREDIENTS

½ cup finely chopped fresh cilantro
½ cup finely chopped fresh flat-leaf parsley
1 tablespoon grated lemon zest
2 garlic cloves, finely chopped
1 tablespoon olive oil
¼ teaspoon Aleppo pepper or crushed red
    pepper flakes
Pinch turmeric

Combine all the ingredients in a small bowl. Rub over the striped bass and let the fish sit for at least 10 minutes or up to 1 day, refrigerated, before grilling.

CUCUMBER TARTAR SAUCE

I love this "tartar sauce." It's definitely different than the stuff that comes in a jar at the grocery store, and its fresh flavor is as unique as it is addictive. At the restaurant we make this so often that the fresh cucumber juice is saved from each batch for our CRU-comber cocktail.

You'll find this sauce makes a perfect accompaniment to any fried, grilled, or baked seafood. It's particularly delicious with grilled striped bass on a summer evening, after a day out on the water. You can leave the skins on the cucumbers or peel them if the skin seems too tough.

INGREDIENTS

2 cucumbers
1 cup mayonnaise
⅓ cup chopped fresh flat-leaf parsley
¼ cup capers, drained
¼ cup sliced pepperoncini
1 preserved lemon, finely chopped, or strips of zest from 1 lemon, very thinly sliced

Slice the cucumbers down the center lengthwise and remove the seeds by running a small spoon down the middle. Grate the cucumbers on a box grater onto a clean kitchen towel. Pull the corners of the towel together and squeeze the towel to remove excess liquid; transfer the cucumbers to a mixing bowl.

Add the mayonnaise, parsley, capers, pepperoncini, and lemon; toss quickly; cover and refrigerate until ready to use. (This sauce will keep 2 to 3 days refrigerated but will quickly lose its freshness. It's best served the day it's made.)

GRILLED LOBSTERS WITH HERB AND CORAL BUTTER

→ SERVES 4 ←

This is such a quintessential Nantucket summertime dish, perfect for an alfresco dinner with family or friends. For the herb butter, feel free to substitute any fresh herbs. If you are lucky enough to get a female lobster with some "coral" or roe inside, it will make a beautiful, and tasty, addition to the butter.

FOR THE LOBSTERS

4 (1½-pound) live lobsters
Kosher salt
2 lemons, cut in half

FOR THE COMPOUND BUTTER

Lobster roe (optional)
1 cup (2 sticks) unsalted butter, softened
1 red Fresno chile, stemmed, seeded, and minced
1 shallot, minced
1 garlic clove, minced
1 tablespoon fresh lemon thyme leaves
2 tablespoons finely chopped fresh chives
1 teaspoon kosher salt
Cracked black pepper

TO PREPARE THE LOBSTERS: Carefully split the lobsters in half lengthwise with a chef's knife, bringing the knife down completely through the head and then through the tail. Pull off the claws and legs from the lobsters and crack the claws slightly with the back of the knife. Rinse the body cavities under cool water. Remove any dark green roe (coral) and set aside in a small bowl. Pat the lobsters dry and refrigerate until you are ready to grill.

(continued)

TO MAKE THE COMPOUND BUTTER: Slightly mash the reserved coral (if using) with a fork. Bring 1 cup of water to a boil and pour over the lobster roe. This will quickly cook the roe, turning it bright pink. Drain the roe in a fine-mesh sieve and transfer to a medium bowl. Add the softened butter, chile, shallot, garlic, lemon thyme, chives, and salt and sprinkle with pepper. Stir to combine.

Preheat the grill to medium-high heat. Season the lobster tails with salt. Place the claws on the grill, cooking each side for about 8 minutes per side. Lay the tails flesh side down for 4 minutes. Flip the tails. Put 1 tablespoon of the compound butter on each tail and cook for 6 more minutes or until the shells turn bright red and are charred in a few places.

Arrange the cooked lobster on a platter. Brush with the remaining butter and serve with the lemon halves.

HOW TO SELECT, TRANSPORT, AND STORE LIVE LOBSTERS

Before you head to the fish market, get a cooler that will accommodate the number of lobsters you want to purchase (without jamming them in); you may need more than one cooler. Arrange a sealable plastic bag of ice cubes in the bottom of the cooler to form a layer of ice about two inches deep and cover it with several layers of newspaper. Place the lid on the cooler. Voilà: you now have a safe way to bring home live lobsters that will still be alive and fresh after the car ride.

Look for lobsters that are actively moving about in the fish market's lobster tank. Avoid any that appear sluggish or that have large barnacles on them.

Some lobster-lovers are convinced that female lobsters have sweeter meat than the males. If you want to see if you agree, you can determine a lobster's sex by looking at the underside of the tail: the females have slightly wider tails than the males, and the shape is also slightly curved when compared to the narrower, straighter tail of the male. You can also ask the staff at the fish market to help you determine a lobster's sex.

Lobsters of one and a half pounds (up to about two pounds) are easiest to handle and an ideal size for most home chefs to cook.

A cull—a lobster missing one claw—is priced at less per pound than lobsters with both claws intact; the flavor of the meat is the same. And lobsters that are molting (when a lobster abandons its old shell and grows a new one), have such tender shells it is extremely easy to remove the meat from them after cooking. The fish market staff can tell you which, if any, of the live lobsters are molting.

Place your live lobsters (with the rubber bands still on the claws!) in your cooler on top of the layers of newspaper, set the lid on the cooler, and place it on the floor of your car. Make buying live lobsters your *last* stop before heading home—visit the farm stand for corn and tomatoes and whatever else you need for your meal *before* you stop at the fish market. You want the lobsters to go from the tank of circulating salt water at the fish market to your fridge (or stockpot) as quickly as possible.

Once home, if you will not be cooking the lobsters right away, store them in the crisper drawer of your refrigerator. Do NOT store the lobsters in water (fresh or salted). The cool temperature of your crisper drawer will keep the lobsters alive but will put them into a sleepy state, which means they won't be thrashing around. Store them this way until you are ready to cook them, which should be the same day you buy them.

Remove the live lobsters from the fridge only when you are ready to drop them into the cooking pot.

Save the cooked lobster bodies and empty shells for lobster bisque; place them in a sealable freezer-safe storage bag and store in the freezer until ready to use.

ZUCCHINI RIBBON SALAD WITH LEMON VINAIGRETTE AND MINT

→ SERVES 6 ←

This recipe is dead-simple. It has morphed over the years depending on what is being served with it. Sliced into long beautiful ribbons on a mandoline, the zucchini is quickly blanched in salted water and shocked to keep the edges bright green.

This composed salad can be beefed up in many ways. Goat cheese, feta, or bits of Pecorino cheese would all be perfectly at home with the zucchini. A few olives, cherry tomatoes, or chiles would be great, too. It can be topped with a wide range of proteins as well, such as grilled shrimp, squid, or lamb chops. Seriously, it goes with everything!

FOR THE LEMON VINAIGRETTE

2 tablespoons grated lemon zest plus
  6 tablespoons juice
1 teaspoon honey
1 teaspoon Dijon mustard
½ teaspoon kosher salt
¾ cup olive oil

FOR THE ZUCCHINI SALAD

1½ pounds zucchini (or summer squash)
1 shallot, thinly sliced
⅓ cup fresh mint leaves
Edible blossoms such as chive blossoms,
  rosemary flowers, sweet pea blossoms
  (pictured), or nasturtiums (optional)

TO MAKE THE VINAIGRETTE: In a large bowl, whisk the lemon zest and juice, honey, mustard, and salt to combine. Slowly whisk in the oil.

TO MAKE THE ZUCCHINI SALAD: Bring a large pot of salted water to a boil. Prepare a bowl of ice water with a sieve next to the stove.

Using a mandoline, cut long, thin strips of zucchini. (If not using a mandoline, cut the zucchini into 4-inch sections and then into thin, even planks.) Blanch the zucchini in the boiling water for 1 to 2 minutes, or until it can bend without breaking. Transfer the zucchini to the ice water. Once it is cool, leave it to drain thoroughly in a large colander lined with a clean kitchen towel.

Add the zucchini and shallot to the vinaigrette. Allow the zucchini to marinate in the vinaigrette for about 10 minutes before adding the mint, edible flowers (if using), and extra lemon zest. Serve immediately.

ALMOND CAKE WITH FRESH PEACHES AND HONEY WHIPPED CREAM

→ MAKES ONE 12-INCH CAKE; SERVES 8 ←

Modeled after the French pastry called a financier, with its browned butter and almond flour, this cake is delicious filled with summer berries or any stone fruit. I even make it with mangoes during the winter months. This cake is great for dessert but it can be served as a coffee cake for brunch, too.

INGREDIENTS

1 cup (2 sticks) butter, plus extra for the pan

6 egg whites

1 teaspoon vanilla paste

2 cups confectioners' sugar

1 cup all-purpose flour

1 cup almond flour

½ teaspoon sea salt

3 peaches, peeled, pitted, and cut into eighths

¼ cup sliced almonds

1 tablespoon coarse sugar (demerara or turbinado)

Honey Whipped Cream (recipe follows)

Preheat the oven to 375°F. Butter and flour a 12-inch tart pan.

In a medium saucepan, cook the butter over medium heat until it begins to brown and smells caramelized. Watch it carefully so that it does not burn! Remove the pan from the heat and let the butter cool to room temperature.

In a large bowl, combine with a wooden spoon or spatula the egg whites and vanilla paste with the room-temperature browned butter. Add the confectioners' sugar, flour, almond flour, and salt and mix thoroughly.

(continued)

Add the cake batter to the tart pan. Arrange the sliced peaches on top of the batter. Sprinkle with the sliced almonds and coarse sugar. Bake for 20 to 25 minutes, or until golden in color and a cake tester inserted in the cake comes out clean.

Transfer to a wire rack and let cool completely before slicing. Top each portion with a dollop of honey whipped cream and serve.

HONEY WHIPPED CREAM

→ **MAKES 2 CUPS** ←

INGREDIENTS

1 cup heavy cream
2 tablespoons honey

Using a mixer with the whisk attachment, whip the cream until it begins to thicken. Add the honey and continue to beat to soft peaks. Chill the whipped cream or use immediately.

BEACH CRUISING

BAREFOOT HOLIDAY

RECIPES FOR
BEACH
CRUISING

Sicilian Caponata and
Fresh Mozzarella Sandwiches

Ham and Brie Baguette with Arugula
and Radishes

Creamy Cucumber Salad

Hazelnut Shortbread with
Wild Blackberry Jam

Nantucket has a beach for every preference. Some attract families with young children; others are favored by the older crowd who prefer an afternoon comfortably reclined with a good book under an umbrella; while others appeal to the twenty-something group listening to loud music and playing beach games. The great variety of beaches on the island allows visitors to experience rolling waves or soft surf, varying light, and unique settings. From the expansive sandbars of Eel Point and Dionis beaches to classic Surfside and Fisherman's beaches (with good bike access, and the Surfside Shack for burgers and dogs) to the bohemian surfer scene at Fat Ladies and Cisco beaches, Nantucket can provide a perfect seashore setting for every liking.

Yet, with all that variety, there is something that all the Nantucket beaches have in common: broad stretches of pristine sand, lovely views, gentle ocean breezes—and room.

Never crowded despite being cited by the Travel Channel as home to "America's best beaches," the island has strands that face virtually every point on the compass. The beaches on the north shore of the island have a gentler surf, suitable for children, with the exception of Brant Point, which has a strong current. The south shore beaches, on the Atlantic side of the island, tend to have cooler water temps than those on the north shore, and heavier surf, too. On the eastern end of the island, quiet inner harbor beaches contrast with 'Sconset beach and its dramatic bluffs.

Whether you seek a setting with billowing masses of beach roses, undulating dunes, or a shoreline that offers the best opportunities for shell-collecting, Nantucket has a beach for you and this chapter celebrates them. After all, beginning in the 1870s, vacationers were drawn to the island for its spectacular, and restorative, "sea-bathing," an activity loved to this day by residents and visitors alike.

We know your beach-cruising adventure will have to include a picnic, so we have put together a classic menu of sandwiches, salad, and dessert that travel well and satisfy a day-at-the-beach appetite. We kept in mind the vegetarian as well as the omnivore as we chose sandwich recipes, and we believe you'll love them both. Wherever your holiday cruising takes you, we think these picnic goodies will become summer go-to favorites.

Long after your Nantucket vacation has drawn to a close, we think you'll be reminiscing about that delicious picnic lunch with friends as much as the stunningly beautiful, soul-renewing beaches of the Faraway Island.

BEACH CRUISING GUIDE

There are so many beautiful beaches on Nantucket, it's good to know a little about your choices before you set off for a day of strolling, lounging, and saltwater swimming. Here's info on nine that suit a range of ages and tastes.

On the island's **north shore**, the beaches face Nantucket Sound, which means the water is warmer and the waves are smaller than at the south shore beaches. For these reasons, families with young children often choose these beaches:

Jetties Beach, at 4 Bathing Beach Road, is an easy walk (or bike ride) from town, and with its shallow, calm water, it's well-suited for young families. Beach chairs and umbrellas can be rented, and there are changing rooms with showers. When everyone is tired of swimming, there are other options: a playground, volleyball nets, and tennis courts. You can even arrange for sailing lessons.

Children's Beach is located off Harbor View Way (across from the Steamboat Wharf in town) and, as its name suggests, this is a popular spot for young families because of its shallow waters and lack of waves.

Brant Point, at 2 Easton Street, is within walking distance of downtown and is a perfect place to lounge and watch sail and motor yachts come and go. For that very reason (heavy boat traffic), plus the fact that there are no lifeguards on this beach, it is not a good choice for swimming. But it is very picturesque. So pretty, as a matter of fact, this beach and the iconic lighthouse at its tip attract photographers and artists.

On the island's **south shore**, the beaches face the Atlantic Ocean, making them ideal for beachgoers who favor surf and don't mind the cooler water. There, you'll find these three beaches:

Surfside, at the end of Surfside Road, is one of the most popular beaches on Nantucket—for locals and visitors. You can get to this beach from a three-mile bike path or via shuttle service from town. Families with older kids and young couples love this beach for its easy access and amenities. Surfside is wide, so you'll find plenty of room to set up camp for your picnic.

Nobadeer, near the airport, is known for its party scene. Not surprisingly, this beach is popular with surfers and college kids. It is also one of the few beaches you can drive on (an attraction for some, a turn-off for others!), so keep that in mind before you head out. This beach has no lifeguards and no rest rooms, so it's not for everyone.

Cisco, on Hummock Pond Road, is a great choice for avid surfers or those who just enjoy watching big dramatic rollers. While you can rent surfboards and stand-up paddle boards here, do so with caution as this stretch is known for strong riptides.

On the island's **east shore**, which meets the Atlantic Ocean, the beaches are known for gorgeous bluffs and long stretches of nearly empty sand. Two beaches here are worth considering:

'Sconset, on Cod Fish Park Road, is picture-postcard pretty. The beach is a little more difficult to get to than others on the island, which means you'll be rewarded with fewer people and a mellow, more grown-up vibe. There tends to be heavy surf and strong currents off the island's east shore beaches but 'Sconset is a lovely choice for the right person. Also known as a great spot for seal-watching.

Great Point, which is off Great Point Road on Wauwinet Road, is a CRU favorite for its gorgeous surroundings of conservation land and water on both sides where the harbor meets the ocean. It's a long beach (seven miles), with Great Point Lighthouse at its end, and the views are lovely. This excellent spot for surfcasting is only accessible by four-wheel drive. Stopping on your way back to town at the Wauwinet Inn for a glass of champagne or hand-crafted painkiller is always a special treat.

On Nantucket's **west shore**, we have an insider's tip and it happens to be the best place on the island to catch the sunset:

Madaket Beach, just off Madaket Road, is where you'll find a beautiful soft-sand beach with lots of privacy. This area is known for dangerous undertows, riptides, and strong surf, though. So, while it's ideal for hanging out for the day with an umbrella and good book, and watching some of the island's best sunsets, it's not so great for someone who likes to be out in the water catching waves.

SICILIAN CAPONATA AND FRESH MOZZARELLA SANDWICHES

→→ SERVES 4 ←←

This is a great sandwich for a picnic, as caponata is always better served at room temperature. The ingredients remind me of the best panini I've ever had. On a small side street in Marsala, Sicily, I ordered a spicy eggplant and fresh mozzarella panini from a roadside caravan. It was incredible! If you're not planning on hitting the road with this sandwich, I highly recommend pressing it and serving it warm.

INGREDIENTS

1 baguette

6 ounces fresh mozzarella, sliced

1½ cups Sicilian Caponata (recipe follows)

¼ cup fresh basil leaves, sliced

Extra-virgin olive oil

Slice the baguette in half lengthwise. Arrange the sliced mozzarella along the length of the bottom half of the baguette. Top with the caponata and basil. Drizzle with a little oil. Set the top half of the baguette in place and slice the sandwich into four portions. Wrap each portion tightly in parchment paper, securing it with a piece of tape. The sandwiches may be kept at room temperature for 2 to 3 hours.

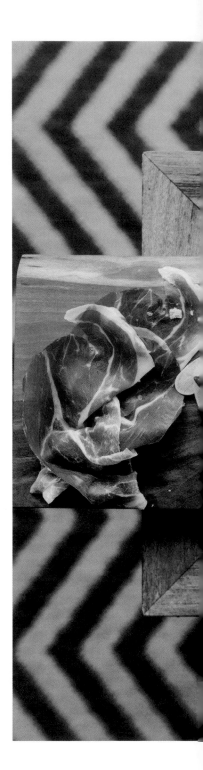

SICILIAN CAPONATA

A few years ago, I spent a month traveling around Sicily. Nearly every restaurant on the island begins each meal with caponata. I immediately fell in love with the play of sweet and sour in this versatile condiment. To me, it is Sicily in one bite with the capers from the neighboring island, the fennel that grows wild, and the eggplant, which seems to be rolling off of every rickety farm truck that goes sputtering by.

INGREDIENTS

½ cup olive oil

1 large eggplant, cut into 1-inch dice

1 celery stalk, sliced

1 small red onion, diced

½ fennel bulb, diced

5 garlic cloves, chopped

½ cup golden raisins

½ teaspoon crushed red pepper flakes

½ cinnamon stick

1½ teaspoons coarsely chopped fresh rosemary

1 cup water

2 tablespoons cider vinegar

2 tablespoons tomato paste

2 tablespoons capers

1 tablespoon sugar

1½ teaspoons kosher salt

Heat the oil in a large 12-inch skillet over medium heat. Add the eggplant and cook until it becomes golden and tender. Add the celery, onion, fennel, and garlic and cook for 2 minutes. Add the raisins, red pepper flakes, cinnamon stick, and rosemary and cook another 2 minutes, stirring often.

In a bowl, whisk together the water, vinegar, tomato paste, capers, sugar, and salt and pour over the eggplant mixture. Lower the heat and let the liquid reduce by half; you want the caponata to be saucy, but not soupy. Remove from the heat and let cool to room temperature before serving.

Or, refrigerate, covered for up to three days, until ready to serve. The caponata, however, is best served at room temperature and tastes even better the next day.

NANTUCKET BY BICYCLE

It's easy to explore Nantucket by bicycle—because it's so small (only fourteen miles from end to end), and because there is not a lot of traffic on the roads and most cars are going only twenty miles an hour, and because there are more than thirty miles of beautifully maintained bike paths. Getting around the island by bike is a sure way to immerse yourself in its magical beauty. Explore the back roads, head to a farmers' market, or use a bike path to discover a beach or visit a museum. Downtown can be crowded during the height of summer but you can easily walk along with your bike, window-shopping, and when the right items beckon, leave your bike outside without worry.

The island caters to discerning tastes, which is reflected even at bicycle rental businesses. At Nantucket Bike Shop on Straight Wharf and Broad Street (a short walk from the ferries), for example, where you can rent a bicycle for an hour, a day, or a week, your choices will include the latest in trail, all-terrain, and hybrid bikes for adults and children, as well as tandem bikes and vintage bikes. And, because this is Nantucket, your bike will come with a handy wicker basket to hold your picnic or your purchases.

A long stay would be required to see all there is to see on the island by bicycle but here are three bike path routes we think you'll want to check out:

• The Hummock Pond loop starts just east of where Cliffs Road intersects with Madaket Road and gives you a scenic six-mile ride with lots of views of the ocean.

• The Barnard Valley Road path gives you a view of the "inland" part of the island. Starting at the intersection of Hoicks Hollow and Polpis Roads, you'll find parts of this three-mile ride quite steep. Worth it, though, to make your way across the moors to Alter Rock, the highest point on Nantucket, with fabulous views in every direction.

• The Polpis Road route winds along marshes, ponds, and the island's cranberry bogs. Lots of good bird-watching opportunities on the route, and the Lifesaving Museum, which is also on this road, is worth a visit.

HAM AND BRIE BAGUETTE WITH ARUGULA AND RADISHES

France definitely has a leg up on the fast-food scene. I love grabbing a sandwich at a corner shop that might have salami and butter or ham and spicy Dijon mustard. Always really simple and never made complicated by anyone's requests. It is what it is and it's always really delicious!

This is a great sandwich to take to a picnic as it's better left at room temperature.

INGREDIENTS

1 baguette

6 ounces brie, room temperature

8 ounces thinly sliced prosciutto or good-quality ham such as Bayonne

2 cups arugula

6 radishes, thinly sliced

Extra-virgin olive oil

2 tablespoons Dijon mustard

Slice the baguette in half lengthwise. Spread the brie as evenly as possible on the bottom half of the baguette. Arrange the ham over the brie. Toss the arugula and radishes with a few drops of oil and arrange over the ham. Spread the mustard on the top half of the baguette and set in place. Slice the sandwich into four portions. Wrap each portion tightly in parchment paper, securing it with a piece of tape. The sandwiches may be kept at room temperature for 2 to 3 hours.

CREAMY CUCUMBER SALAD

This salad was one of my childhood favorites. My mother and her twin sister would make it all summer long when the cucumbers were coming in nonstop from the garden. Slightly sweet with a delicious, light, creamy dressing, this chilled dish is perfect with a crispy piece of panko-crusted bluefish or striped bass—which is how I like to serve it at the restaurant. At home, I'll keep a batch in the fridge for lunches, snacking, or taking to the beach. Serve this salad well chilled.

INGREDIENTS

4 cucumbers
Kosher salt
1 white onion, thinly sliced
⅓ cup apple cider vinegar
¼ cup sugar
1 cup mayonnaise
¼ cup sour cream
3 tablespoons chopped fresh dill
¼ teaspoon freshly ground black pepper

Peel the cucumbers, cut in half lengthwise, and scoop out the seeds. Cut them into ¼-inch slices. Place the sliced cucumbers in a colander and toss with 1 teaspoon salt. Let them sit for 15 minutes to leach out excess moisture, then lightly press them to release as much liquid as possible.

Meanwhile, combine the onion, vinegar, sugar, and 2 teaspoons salt in a large bowl. Stir to dissolve the sugar, then add the mayonnaise, sour cream, dill, and pepper. Add the cucumbers and toss gently. Cover and refrigerate until ready to serve.

NOTE: You can replace the cucumbers in this recipe with two European, or English, cucumbers. You won't need to peel or seed them; simply wash, slice, and go. You can skip the colander and salt step, too.

HAZELNUT SHORTBREAD WITH WILD BLACKBERRY JAM

This is my absolute favorite of all the cookies my grandmother, Fern, used to make. I adore hazelnuts and the little bit of salt with the sweet makes these simple cookies perfectly balanced. Here on Nantucket, blackberries grow wild. I have enough behind my house to make a few batches of blackberry jam every summer, my favorite accompaniment to these cookies. An excellent alternative to blackberry jam is Nantucket beach plum jam.

INGREDIENTS

1 cup (2 sticks) unsalted butter
1 cup sugar
2 cups all-purpose flour
8 ounces hazelnuts, toasted, skinned, and ground
½ teaspoon kosher salt
½ cup homemade or store-bought blackberry jam

In a mixer with the paddle attachment, cream the butter and sugar until light and fluffy. Add the flour, ground hazelnuts, and salt and mix until evenly incorporated. Form the dough into a ball, wrap tightly in plastic wrap, and refrigerate for at least 2 hours or, better yet, overnight. (The dough may also be frozen and thawed before use.)

Preheat the oven to 350°F. Remove the dough from the refrigerator and divide in two. Roll one piece of dough between two sheets of waxed paper to about ⅓ inch thick. (Using waxed paper is helpful as the dough is a bit crumbly and sticky.) Cut out rounds with a small cookie or 2-inch biscuit cutter and place them on a parchment paper–lined baking sheet. Repeat with the second piece of dough.

Bake the cookies for 8 to 10 minutes, until just set. Do not let them brown.

Gently remove the cookies from the baking sheet and transfer to a wire rack. Let them cool completely. Spread the jam on half of the cookies and top with the remaining cookies.

COCKTAILS IN THE BACK BAR

ENJOYING THE JOVIALITY OF SPIRITS

One of life's simple pleasures is meeting up with friends at the end of the day for a cocktail. Whether it's a prelude to dinner or the center of a let's-play-it-by-ear evening of small plates, there's something celebratory about raising a toast with a well-prepared drink served in a beautiful glass.

At CRU Oyster Bar Nantucket, Carlos Hidalgo has elevated the art of the cocktail to its deserved status: fine spirits are combined with thoughtful inventiveness to suit the time of year and the cuisine du jour. He and his staff have created a drinks menu that tips its hat to your favorite classics while simultaneously departing from tradition to focus on local seasonal fruits, vegetables, and herbs. "We're proud of the fact that CRU was one of the first on the island to adopt the 'farm-to-glass' approach," he says. Locally grown chamomile shows up in the Lady Juju; just-picked strawberries distinguish the Valentina; and fresh-from-the-vine cucumbers make the CRUcomber exceptionally refreshing. Naturally enough, the cocktail menu changes to reflect the season.

The results are fragrant, jewel-colored, perfectly chilled concoctions that are pleasing to all the senses, precisely why the cocktails at CRU have been extolled in *Travel & Leisure*, *Food & Wine*, and other leading publications.

Now, with this collection of a baker's dozen of never-before-published recipes for elegant drinks, you can re-create the marvelous experience of sipping a cocktail at CRU Oyster Bar Nantucket. Cheers!

Note: We are listing the brands we use in these recipes, some of which your local liquor store may not carry. Talk to a knowledgeable salesperson to find out what makes for good substitutes.

RECIPES FOR
COCKTAILS
IN THE BACK BAR

The Valentina

CRU Spicy Bloody Mary

CRUcomber

Amore Americano

Salty Mutt

LP #02554

Billyburg

Bienvenue!

Kentucky Monk

Hey, Jealousy

Rio Calling

Lady Juju

Naughty and Nice

THE VALENTINA

This cocktail is a perfect late-spring into summer libation. Its deep pink color and bright green garnish are a salute to the seasons, as is its fresh taste.

On Nantucket, strawberry season begins in mid-May. Inspired by the fragrance and sweet-tart taste of the berries, Carlos Hidalgo wanted to develop a cocktail that would showcase them without being one-dimensional or sweet. He pulled it off in spades with the Valentina; the freshness of lime, the subtle heat of habanero-infused tequila, and the peppery sweet bite of basil give this drink a savory depth that does not detract from the luscious fresh fruitiness of the strawberries.

Cheers to the season that kicks off CRU's year, and to the pleasure of sipping a cocktail out of doors with friends, enjoying the waterfront—or whatever your view may be.

INGREDIENTS

6 fresh strawberries, hulled

2 fresh basil leaves, plus extra for garnish

5 ounces habanero-infused Don Julio Blanco Tequila (recipe follows),
   or tequila of your choice

1½ ounces fresh lime juice

½ ounce agave syrup

Slice 2 habanero peppers
   (You may use red or red and orange peppers.)

Place peppers inside the tequila for 24 to 36 hours.

The infusion time will dictate the level of spice you would like for your spicy tequila. When the desired heat level is achieved, strain the tequila, removing all seeds and peppers.

Muddle the strawberries and basil leaves in a metal shaker. Add the tequila, lime juice, and agave. Shake vigorously and double strain into the table side of an ice shaker. Serve in a coupe glass with a basil leaf garnish.

CRU SPICY BLOODY MARY

Our house Bloody Mary is the perfect accompaniment to pristine seafood. Created by Carlos Hidalgo to complement CRU's flavorful, icy-cold, and perfectly shucked oysters, this drink has a spicy depth of flavor that brightens any brunch.

Yes, our Bloody Mary mix calls for a lot of ingredients, but you'll make it a day in advance. When your guests arrive, you'll have very little to do. Enjoy!

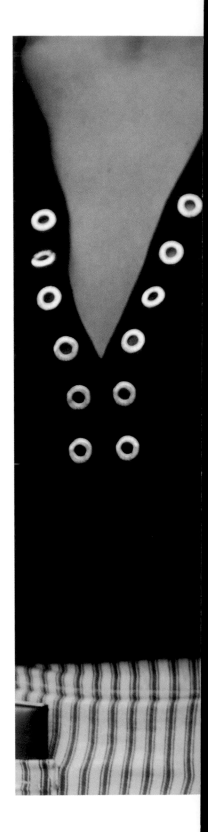

FOR THE BLOODY MARY MIX

2 quarts (8 cups) tomato juice
½ cup fresh lemon juice
6 tablespoons Worcestershire sauce
¼ cup wasabi powder
3 tablespoons grated horseradish
3 tablespoons fresh lime juice
2 tablespoons grated fresh ginger
2 tablespoons sugar
2 tablespoons garlic powder
1½ tablespoons celery seeds
1½ tablespoons freshly ground black pepper
1½ tablespoons crushed red pepper flakes
1½ tablespoons kosher salt
1½ tablespoons onion powder

FOR THE SPICY BLOODY MARYS

Ice cubes
24 ounces vodka
12 caper berries
12 pepperoncini
12 lemon wedges

TO MAKE THE BLOODY MARY MIX: Combine all the ingredients in a large pitcher and stir well. Cover and refrigerate overnight (this step allows the flavors to meld and come to life).

TO MAKE THE SPICY BLOODY MARYS: Fill 12 Collins glasses with ice. Into each glass pour 2 ounces vodka and add ¾ cup Bloody Mary mix. Garnish each drink with a caper berry, a pepperoncini, and a lemon wedge. Serve.

CRUCOMBER

Our signature cocktail has a bright freshness we crave all summer long. Zubrowska Bison Grass Vodka is flavored with one strand of grass and has notes of coconut and quinine. It's quite delicious and worth hunting for if your local liquor store doesn't carry it.

A beautiful green color from the cucumbers, this cocktail is the epitome of thirst-quenching at the end of a long summer day. Caution: as CRU's own Kat Dunn (creator of the recipe) warns, "You could easily drink it by the pitcher . . ." Also note that you need to make the Toasted Sesame Simple Syrup a day in advance.

INGREDIENTS

1 fresh cucumber (peeled and chopped),
   plus 1 unpeeled cucumber sliced for garnish
2 lemon balm or lemon verbena leaves
1½ ounces fresh lemon juice
1½ ounces Toasted Sesame Simple Syrup (recipe follows)
5 ounces Zubrowska Bison Grass Vodka (or vodka of your choice)
Crushed ice

Puree the prepared cucumbers in a blender with a small amount of water. Strain through a fine-mesh sieve and set aside.

Slap lemon balm leaves to release their essence and place in a cocktail shaker. Add cucumber puree, lemon juice, and sesame syrup. Add vodka and crushed ice; shake vigorously. Double strain into a pitcher to filter out any cucumber residue. Serve straight up in a coupe, or on the rocks, garnished with cucumber slices.

TOASTED SESAME SIMPLE SYRUP

→ MAKES 1 CUP ←

INGREDIENTS

½ cup water

½ cup sugar

¼ cup white sesame seeds,
   toasted until deep golden brown

Place the water in a small saucepan and bring to a boil. Add the sugar and stir until dissolved. Add the toasted sesame seeds while still hot (directly from the oven) to the syrup. Transfer the mixture to a glass jar with a tight-fitting lid and let stand overnight. The next day, pour through a fine-mesh sieve to remove the seeds.

THE WELL-STOCKED LIQUOR CABINET

If you're just beginning to appreciate the fun of cocktails (perhaps beer or wine has always been your go-to drink), prepare to enter a world of dizzying choices as you stock your liquor cabinet. You'll now be shopping in the section of the liquor store that you've ignored, where row upon row of distilled spirits and liqueurs and bitters and aperitifs and digestifs and *amaros* and distilled wines beckon. Where to begin?

We recommend that you start with a few basics and gradually build a more expanded collection. A good gin, whiskey, rum, tequila, and vodka are five spirits that will allow you to make nearly any popular cocktail. Brand? The recipes in this chapter name most of the spirits by brand but you can also consult with the store's staff and, the next time you're at your favorite bar, ask the bartender for a few of his or her favorite picks.

Don't buy huge bottles; you'll have to wait too long for the opportunity to try another brand. As you establish your collection, you want to be able to experiment and find what suits your palate.

Vermouth, sweet and dry, should be part of your foundation, as should a bottle of Angostura bitters. A good cognac, a bottle of Campari, perhaps a Grand Marnier will likely come in handy. Club soda and tonic (in small bottles, so they won't have time to go flat) are musts for many basic drinks.

As you try cocktail recipes that are new to you, you'll learn which ones are most appealing to your tastes. If gin-based drinks are your favorites, seek out finer brands along with the most commonly called-for ingredients in three good recipes. If whiskey cocktails suit you, you can begin a collection of bourbon, rye, and scotch. For some, one brand of vodka covers all needs. It's all about personal preference. Build a collection of good quality spirits for the kind of drinks you and your friends enjoy.

AMORE AMERICANO

A film about an Italian professor who falls in love with his American assistant . . . The title lends itself to this cocktail because rye whiskey is as quintessential a spirit to America as amaro is to Italy. The amaro softens the bite of the rye, the chamomile adds smooth floral notes, while the bitters balance the sweet vanilla.

As the drink's creator, Jess Goldfarb, says, "The Amore Americano is perfect for CRU because, as a lighter whiskey cocktail, it drinks just as well during the day as it does at sunset or into the night hours."

INGREDIENTS

Large (2-inch square) ice cubes
4 ounces Chamomile-Infused Rye (recipe follows)
½ ounce Montenegro Amaro
½ ounce Vanilla Bean Syrup (recipe follows)
3 dashes aromatic bitters
2 strips lemon zest, twisted

Add ice cubes to two rocks glasses. Combine the rye, Montenegro Amaro, vanilla syrup, and bitters in a pitcher, mix well, and divide among the glasses. Garnish each drink with a fresh lemon twist and serve.

CHAMOMILE-INFUSED RYE

If you're not a fan of chamomile, skip this step and simply use rye whiskey; you'll still have a delicious cocktail.

INGREDIENTS

¼ cup loose-leaf chamomile tea
4 cups Old Overholt Rye (or rye whiskey of your choice)

Place the chamomile leaves in a 1-quart container or sealable jar. Pour in the rye. Cover and let infuse for 3 hours. Strain the infusion through a fine sieve or cheesecloth into a container and discard the chamomile.

THE RIGHT GLASSWARE

A collection of a few high-ball, old-fashioned, rocks, coupe, and martini glasses will put you in good shape to serve virtually any cocktail. Cocktail recipes will always specify the type of glass a drink should be served in; using the right glass shows off the drink's color, properly holds the volume of a single serving, and in the case of stemware like a coupe or martini glass, keeps your hands from warming the icy-cold but "straight-up" concoction.

VANILLA BEAN SYRUP

→ MAKES 4 CUPS ←

INGREDIENTS

1 vanilla bean
2 cups sugar
2 cups water

Split the vanilla bean lengthwise and scrape the inside into a medium saucepan; add the sugar and water. Bring to a boil over medium-high heat, stirring. When the sugar has dissolved, remove the pan from the heat. Let cool at room temperature. Transfer to a jar with a tight-fitting lid and refrigerate for 24 hours. Strain the syrup through a fine-mesh sieve to remove the vanilla bean, and refrigerate until ready to use.

ICE RULES

Automatic ice makers in refrigerators for the home kitchen are notorious for producing ice with an off-taste. Use that ice for chilling a bottle of wine or champagne in an ice bucket, or for filling a tub designed to hold bottles of beer at a cookout, but not for making cocktails or serving a drink on the rocks. Invest in some good-quality ice-cube trays with lids and keep at least three in your freezer, fresh and ready to use. You'll find plenty to choose from, particularly at shops that specialize in kitchen and bar tools. In addition to trays that make the standard one-inch by two-inch rectangular cube, there are ice cube trays that make large (two-inch by two-inch) squares, trays that produce large spheres of ice, or star- or other novelty-shaped ice. When a drink is served on the rocks, the size and shape of the ice makes a visual impression. The important thing, though, is that your ice is fresh and flavorless.

SALTY MUTT

The Salty Dog is a staple drink on the New England coast and islands. That fact, and because we love the refreshing aspects of a Shandy, we thought a hybrid would pair excellently with CRU's menu and appeal to our customers. Hence the name Salty Mutt. The grapefruit and fennel work well together while the vodka adds a bit of a kick and the gin's botanicals round out the citrus and crispness of the beer. As CRU's Jess Goldfarb likes to point out, "The other beauty of this drink: during those sweltering hot days of summer, one can just get a larger glass and add more beer." Bottoms up!

INGREDIENTS

Fennel Sea Salt (recipe follows)
½ ounce fresh lemon juice
1 ounce Absolut Ruby Red Vodka (or vodka of your choice)
1 ounce Hendricks Gin (or gin of your choice)
1 ounce St-Germain
½ ounce fresh grapefruit juice
12 dashes grapefruit bitters
Lagunitas Pilsner, or other American-style pilsner

Pour the fennel salt into a shallow dish. Moisten the rims of two highball glasses with a little lemon juice; dip half of each rim into the salt.

Combine the remaining lemon juice, the vodka, gin, St-Germain, grapefruit juice, and bitters and shake. Strain over ice into the highball glasses, leaving room. Top each drink with pilsner. Serve.

FENNEL SEA SALT

2 tablespoons fennel seeds
2 tablespoons kosher salt
½ teaspoon sea salt

Grind the fennel seeds in a spice grinder until coarse. Transfer to a lidded jar and add the salts. Cover and shake until the mixture is evenly blended.

LP #02554

The name of this drink is a take on Love Potion Number Nine—but with the Nantucket ZIP code swapped in. "It's always good to have a rum-inspired drink when on an island, no matter whether the island is in the Caribbean or New England," says Jess Goldfarb. "I wanted a rum drink that had good fruit without being too sweet. That's why I used Rhum Clement, which is an *agricole*-style rum, meaning no added molasses. Smoking the pineapple dries out some of the residual sugars while the bitters helps balance out the syrup."

INGREDIENTS

½ ounce Aperol
Ice cubes
3½ ounces Rhum Clement (or rum of your choice)
1 ounce smoked pineapple
½ ounce orgeat syrup
½ ounce lime juice
2 long dashes Angostura bitters
Fresh mint sprigs

Divide the Aperol between two highball glasses and fill each with ice. Combine the rum, smoked pineapple, orgeat syrup, and lime juice in a shaker and shake well; strain into the glasses and top with dashes of bitters. Slap mint in the palm of your hand to release aromas and place as garnish and serve.

BILLYBURG

Inspired by CRU's raw bar, the Billyburg is the creation of Jess Goldfarb. "I thought it would be cool to create a drink that would not only complement the raw bar, but also incorporate it. That's why there is mignonette mist in this cocktail." The aromatics from Greenhook Gin combined with thyme and lemon create a bright, vibrant cocktail that's perfect with oysters and all the raw bar offerings.

The name of this drink—in honor of the home of Greenhook Gin (Williamsburg, a borough of New York City referred to by New Yorkers as Billyburg)—is as fun to say as the cocktail is to imbibe.

INGREDIENTS

4 ounces Greenhook Gin (or gin of your choice)
1½ ounces fresh lemon juice
1½ ounces Thyme Syrup (recipe follows)
½ ounce Cocchi Americano
4 grinds of freshly ground black pepper per serving
Mignonette (page 26), strained into a small mister
Fresh sage leaves

Pour the gin, lemon juice, thyme syrup, and Cocchi Americano into a shaker over ice. Shake well.

Spritz a coupe glass with a little mignonette mist. Immediately double strain the cocktail into the glass. Slap sage leaf on hand to release aroma and place as garnish. Add 2 grinds of pepper before serving.

THYME SYRUP

INGREDIENTS

1 cup water
1 cup sugar
4 thyme sprigs

Combine the water and sugar in a small saucepan. Bring to a boil over medium-high heat, stirring. When the sugar has dissolved, remove the pan from the heat. Add the thyme sprigs and let cool to room temperature; strain and store in the refrigerator.

A two-part metal shaker is my recommendation for recipes that call for shaking the ingredients. The jigger (a measuring cup created for making mixed drinks), is really a must-have because it allows you to measure the liquids easily and accurately, unlike a shot glass. The strainer fits into the top of one of your shakers and allows you to pour the cocktail while leaving the ice (and things like herbs or other ingredients used for flavor) behind.

For cocktails that are stirred not shaken— like a classic martini or Manhattan—you need what is called a mixing glass. The bar spoon is a long-handled spoon that's ideal for stirred drinks made in the mixing glass. The muddler is a long utensil with a wide blunted end that can be used in the mixing glass for smashing herbs or fruit or mixing in sugar.

If you like to entertain by offering your guests a choice of two cocktails, a couple of attractive glass cocktail pitchers are good to have. In many cases, you can combine the drink's ingredients shortly before your guests arrive, pour it into a pitcher, and store in your fridge (cover the top of the pitcher with plastic wrap) until you are ready to pour. Use your bar spoon to give the mixture a stir before pouring.

You don't need a lot of fancy equipment to begin making elegant cocktails at home but you do need a few basics. A cocktail shaker, jigger, and strainer will get you started. To complete your barware, you'll want just a few more items: a mixing glass, a bar spoon, and a muddler.

BIENVENUE!

This drink was designed to be served as an aperitif—clean, crisp, and refreshing—something to get your mouth watering before dinner.

INGREDIENTS

2 ounces Svedka Citron Vodka (or other citrus vodka of your choice)

½ ounce Reyka Vodka (or vodka of your choice)

½ ounce Dolin Dry Vermouth (or dry vermouth of your choice)

½ ounce Cocchi Americano

Splash of tonic

1 ounce Moscato per glass

3 spritzes Grape Mist per glass (recipe follows)

3 skewered red grapes per glass

Pour the citrus vodka, vodka, vermouth, and Cocchi Americano into a shaker over ice. Shake well, strain into a port glass, add a splash of tonic and top with 1 ounce Moscato. Finish with 3 spritzes of grape mist. Garnish with skewered grapes. Repeat steps for second glass. Serve.

GRAPE MIST

If you don't want to make this recipe from scratch, you can buy Concord grape juice instead.

INGREDIENTS

4 cups Concord grapes

4 cups white sugar

4 cups water

Place the grapes in a large saucepan and crush them. Add the sugar and water and bring to a boil over medium-high heat; lower the heat and simmer for 10 minutes, stirring occasionally. Let cool, then strain the juice into a container and discard the spent grapes. Cover and refrigerate. When ready to use, place in an atomizer.

KENTUCKY MONK

This cocktail celebrates all of CRU's Kat Dunn's favorite things in a glass. "The name seemed obvious, as Bulleit is a Kentucky bourbon and both the Green Chartreuse and Benedictine are made by monks. The Aperol: just delicious."

INGREDIENTS

3½ ounces Bulleit Bourbon (or bourbon of your choice)

1¾ ounces Green Chartreuse

1 ounce Benedictine

1½ ounces Aperol

2 strips grapefruit zest, plus 2 strips grapefruit zest, twisted, for garnish

1 dash orange bitters

Stir all ingredients with ice (to fill) in a crystal mixing glass for 45 rotations. Using a julep strainer, strain into a tableside shaker. Pour into a coupe glass, garnish with a long grapefruit twist, splash orange bitters on each and serve.

HEY, JEALOUSY

Another inventive creation by CRU's Kat Dunn, this drink was dreamed up while driving from Brooklyn to Nantucket when a Gin Blossoms song by this name came on, inspiring a great cocktail. "It had to be a riff on a Gin Blossom cocktail (gin, apricot eau-de-vie, St-Germain), and as jealousy and bitterness go hand in hand, this drink needed just a touch of Campari. This delicious cocktail starts strong and slightly sweet and ends boozy and slightly bitter."

INGREDIENTS

3½ ounces The Botanist Gin (or gin of your choice)
1½ ounces Cocchi Americano (or Lillet Blanc)
1 ounce St-Germain
4 dashes orange bitters
1 lemon
Campari float (a scant ¼ ounce per glass once poured)

Add the gin, Cocchi Americano, St-Germain, and orange bitters to a mixing glass with ice and stir for 40 rotations. Strain into a coupe glass. Zest a long lemon peel into each glass. Pour the Campari into each glass and serve.

RIO CALLING

The name of this cocktail is a riff on the Clash's "London Calling." When on vacation in Rio, Carlos Hidalgo watched merchants set up their booths and muddle fresh fruit and spices to create the perfect Caipirinha. Inspired, here's his take on Rio's famed cocktail—with a Nantucket spin.

INGREDIENTS

Crushed ice
16 raspberries (a generous 1 cup)
2 whole cloves
5 ounces Leblon Cachaça (or Cachaça of your choice)
2 ounces fresh lime juice
½ ounce ginger syrup
2 lime wheels (round lime slices)

Fill two Collins glasses with crushed ice. Muddle the raspberries and cloves in a shaker. Add the Cachaça, lime juice, and ginger syrup. Shake vigorously and double strain into the glasses. Garnish with the lime wheels and serve.

LADY JUJU

Oh, Lady St. Petsois Juju! This drink, created by Kat Dunn named by Jane Stoddard, screams spring on Nantucket. It is CRU's take on a classic cocktail: the Bee's Knees (gin, lemon, honey). The black pepper gives it a bit of a kick.

INGREDIENTS

6 ounces Pumpkin Pond Farm chamomile–
   infused Citadelle gin (or London Dry Gin or
   gin of your choice)
2 ounces fresh lemon juice

1 ounce egg whites
1 ounce Nantucket honey
Freshly ground black pepper
Edible flowers, such as violets

Add all ingredients (except pepper and flowers!!) to a shaker and shake vigorously. Add ice and shake slightly less vigorously. Double strain into a coupe glass. Garnish with freshly ground black pepper and edible flowers. Serve.

CHAMOMILE-INFUSED GIN

If you're not a fan of chamomile, skip this step and simply use gin; you'll still have a delicious cocktail.

INGREDIENTS

4 good-quality chamomile tea bags or 5 dried chamomile flowers
1 (750-ml) bottle Citadelle gin (or London Dry Gin or gin of your choice)

Add the chamomile to a bottle of gin. Let it steep at room temperature for at least 3 hours. (If using the dried chamomile flowers, let it steep at room temperature for 6 hours.)

NAUGHTY AND NICE

If an espresso martini and a Negroni had a baby, this cocktail from Kat Dunn would be it. The combination of gin, Carpano Antica with its vanilla overtones infused with coffee, and the bitter orange of the Campari make a perfect drink for the crisp air of fall on Nantucket.

INGREDIENTS

3 ounces Beefeater Gin (or gin of your choice)
1½ ounces coffee-infused Carpano Antica (recipe below)
1½ ounces Campari
2 long strips orange zest

Combine the gin, Carpano Antica, and Campari in a mixing glass. Stir for 40 rotations. Strain over fresh ice.

Heat the orange zest with a lighter or long match until it begins to shine from the oils being released. Then, squeeze the orange zest into the flame (you'll know you did it correctly if you see a fire-burst from the zest). Drop the zest into the drink and serve.

COFFEE-INFUSED CARPANO ANTICA

INGREDIENTS

¼ cup of Arabica coffee beans to a bottle of Carpano Antica
Or
1 ounce of Carpano Antica
¼ ounce of canned nitro coffee

Let it sit for an hour at room temperature. Strain coffee beans out.

A DAY ON THE WATER

THE LIVING IS EASY

Nantucket attracts sailors from around the world. The hailing ports identified on the gleaming transoms of sail and motor yachts moored in the harbor tell the tale (the Bahamas; Scotland; France; Denmark; Seattle, Washington; Annapolis, Maryland; Oyster Bay, New York), and during the peak of summer, read like an atlas. Multi-decked superyachts, some with helipads, are not an uncommon sight.

A day spent boating in Nantucket Sound, or circumnavigating the island and dropping anchor off one of the more than a dozen beaches to laze away the afternoon, is a must-do activity for those who enjoy boating, and a great way to see the island from another vantage point. Nantucket's yacht clubs offer boats that can be chartered, with or without a captain.

For avid sailors, these waters are considered some of the best. The currents, depth, wind patterns, and orientation on the compass make for endless days of exhilarating blue-water sailing or laidback cruising close to the coast.

Members of the Barton & Gray Mariners Club can enjoy brunch at CRU and then stroll a few feet to the dock (in front of CRU's outdoor lounge) where two classic Hinckley boats from the Barton & Gray Mariners Club tie up for the season, awaiting mariners. Lunch on the boat can be provided by CRU, the official caterer for all Barton & Gray boating events on Nantucket.

At the end of a day on the water, drinks and lighter fare at CRU Oyster Bar Nantucket are the perfect way to unwind in the lingering glow of the late-summer sun. It's summertime on Nantucket, and the living is easy.

RECIPES FOR
A DAY ON THE WATER

Carrot Hummus

Smoked Fish Dip

Roast Beef Sandwiches with Cambozola
and Pickled Red Onions

Fresh Sliced Melon

Sliced Summer Tomatoes with
Green Goddess Dressing

NANTUCKET'S LIGHTHOUSES

As small as it is—fourteen miles from end to end—Nantucket has three lighthouses. The island's location in the middle of some of the most traversed waters off New England necessitated the lights, and each is still in service.

BRANT POINT LIGHT

The oldest of the three island lighthouses is Brant Point Lighthouse, set at the entrance to Nantucket Harbor. If you travel to Nantucket by ferry, it will be one of the first things you see as the boat approaches the wharf. With a twenty-six-foot-tall tower, Brant Point Lighthouse is the shortest in New England and is so diminutive that, when first sighted, you may wonder if it is a real lighthouse or a charming replica there.

Built in 1746, Brant Point was the second lighthouse in the Colonies. Originally constructed of wood, the lighthouse had to be rebuilt a number of times due to fire and storms, and was eventually replaced with a brick tower. But even that structure succumbed to a storm; in 1901 a new wooden lighthouse was built to replace it, at a location six hundred feet away from the original spot.

It is an island tradition to toss a penny in the water from your departing ferry as you pass the Brant Point Lighthouse. Folklore has it that is the only way to ensure you will return to the magical island again in the future.

SANKATY HEAD LIGHT

Set on the easternmost end of the island in picturesque 'Sconset, on a ninety-foot-high bluff, Sankaty Head Lighthouse stands seventy feet tall. The last lighthouse to be built on Nantucket (construction began in 1849 and ended in 1850), Sankaty Head Light was the first US lighthouse to be outfitted with a Fresnel lens, making it the most powerful light in New England and visible to mariners twenty miles away. That lens was replaced by aerobeacons in 1950 and is part of an exhibit at the Nantucket Whaling Museum.

In 2007, based on predictions of erosion to the cliff, the lighthouse was moved four hundred feet, but the building you see today is, amazingly, the original brick and granite structure, painted white with a broad red stripe.

GREAT POINT LIGHT

Great Point Lighthouse stands at the windswept northernmost point of the island, where, more than two hundred years after it was built, the light still aids mariners traveling between Nantucket and the mainland. Built in 1784 as a wooden tower, it was rebuilt of stone in 1818 after it was destroyed by a fire. That structure had to be replaced in 1986, but it remains a striking replica of the original building, including its exterior stones.

The lighthouse's white sixty-foot tower rises above the grasslands that surround it within the stunningly beautiful Coskata-Coatue Wildlife Refuge. The best way to visit this island gem is via a four-wheel-drive vehicle with a beach permit. There are guided tours that will take you to the top of the tower—a must-do during your visit to Nantucket.

CARROT HUMMUS

When writing the opening menus for CRU, I knew I wanted a sharable vegetarian appetizer, a crowd-pleaser of sorts. We figured that nearly everyone loves hummus. This started a crusade to make it slightly more interesting and ended with us making lots of different veggie-based hummus recipes. The first year was carrot and then we rolled through parsnips, autumn squashes, roasted beets, zucchini, and sweet peas. We serve our hummus with a whole-grain flatbread, olives, and lots of gorgeous crudités.

INGREDIENTS

6 carrots coarsely chopped (4 cups)

1 (15-ounce) can chickpeas, drained (or 2 cups home-cooked chickpeas)

½ cup tahini

6 tablespoons fresh lemon juice

4 garlic cloves

2 teaspoons kosher salt

1 teaspoon ground cumin

Olive oil

Black dry-cured olives, pitted

Coarsely chopped fresh mint leaves

Place the carrots in a medium saucepan, cover with water, and bring to a boil; lower the heat and simmer for about 10 minutes or until completely tender. Add the chickpeas to the carrots for the last 5 minutes of cooking. (Heating the chickpeas makes a smoother hummus.)

Thoroughly drain the carrots and chickpeas and transfer to a large bowl. Add the tahini, lemon juice, garlic, salt, and cumin and puree the mixture, in batches, using a food processor. Transfer to a serving bowl and top the hummus with a drizzle of oil, a scattering of olives, and a handful of mint leaves. Serve.

SMOKED FISH DIP

While I truly love a classic New England bluefish dip that is traditionally bound with cream cheese, our Floribbean version at CRU is a little lighter and brighter. During the summer we have a nonstop rotation of bluefish for our fish dip, from fresh to cured to smoked.

Smoked bluefish can be purchased at most fish markets but if it isn't available, any hot-smoked fish can be substituted here. If you will be smoking the bluefish at home, be sure to cure it for a day or two beforehand in a mixture of salt and sugar. This step helps remove excess moisture from the fish, concentrating its flavor and firming its texture.

Serve this dip with cucumber slices, crackers, or toasted bread.

INGREDIENTS

½ cup white wine vinegar

¼ cup diced white onion

¼ cup diced fennel

½ red or green jalapeño, seeded and minced

1½ pounds smoked bluefish

½ cup plus 2 tablespoons mayonnaise

¼ cup chopped cilantro leaves and stems

1 tablespoon fresh lemon juice

¼ teaspoon curry powder

Kosher salt

Place the vinegar, onion, fennel, and jalapeño in a small saucepan over medium-high heat. Watching closely, simmer the mixture until the vinegar is completely absorbed by the vegetables. Immediately remove from the heat and set aside to cool.

Clean the smoked bluefish by removing any bones, dark bloodline, and skin. (It's important to do a thorough job; bones are not welcome, nor is the fish skin. Removing the dark bloodline will result in a lighter and more delicate fish dip.) Break up the cleaned bluefish into small pieces. Transfer to a food processor and add the pickled vegetables, mayonnaise, cilantro, lemon juice, and curry powder. Pulse just until the ingredients come together; the mixture should be smooth enough to spread but not so processed it resembles a puree. Season to taste with salt.

Transfer to a serving dish, cover tightly with plastic wrap, and refrigerate for at least two hours or until ready to serve. This dip will keep (tightly covered and refrigerated) for up to 1 week.

ROAST BEEF SANDWICHES WITH CAMBOZOLA AND PICKLED RED ONIONS

Life can't get much better than a day on the water with friends, but these roast beef sandwiches will certainly take it up a notch. Rosemary focaccia is the perfect vehicle for the thinly sliced rare beef, creamy pungent blue cheese, and the sweet crunch of pickled red onion. If the funky bite of Cambozola isn't for you, brie, camembert, or cheddar cheese will work beautifully in its place. Or skip the cheese and use our Horseradish Crème Fraîche (page 25) in its place.

INGREDIENTS

1 (2½- to 3-pound) eye of round beef roast

1 teaspoon grapeseed oil or olive oil

2 tablespoons kosher salt

1 tablespoon freshly ground black pepper

1 loaf rosemary focaccia or any rustic bread such as ciabatta or good sourdough

8 ounces Cambozola (or other soft ripened cheese)

Pickled Red Onions (page 252)

1 large bunch watercress or arugula, washed, large stems removed

Dry the roast well, rub with the oil, and then liberally coat with the salt and pepper. Let the beef rest at room temperature for 1 to 2 hours.

Set a large cast-iron skillet in the oven and preheat the oven to 475°F. Place the roast in the hot skillet, being careful not to burn your hands, and bake for 25 to 30 minutes or until the internal temperature of the meat reaches 118°F to 120°F. Remove the skillet from the oven and transfer the beef (gently, with tongs not a fork) to a plate to cool completely. Once cool, wrap tightly in plastic wrap and refrigerate overnight. (Chilling the roast well makes it easier to slice as thinly as possible.)

Slice the beef thinly. Cut the focaccia in half horizontally and spread the Cambozola cheese over the bottom half. Layer beef over the cheese, and over that distribute the pickled onions and watercress. Place the top half of the focaccia on the watercress, press lightly, and cut into the number of sandwiches you need for your group.

Wrap each sandwich tightly in parchment paper and secure with tape before packing for your picnic.

HINCKLEY YACHTS— A LEGACY OF BEAUTY, CRAFTSMANSHIP, AND EXCELLENCE

During the season, the sight of Hinckley yachts in Nantucket Harbor or the Sound is not unusual. The elegance, quality, and sea-readiness of these renowned boats make them perfectly suited to the discerning tastes of those who summer on Nantucket.

Founded by Benjamin Hinckley in 1928 in Southwest Harbor, Maine, the company has been building boats that are admired and owned by yachtsmen around the world for nearly one hundred years. While today we think of a Hinckley as a high-end luxury boat—each boat is built to order with the exterior and interior customized to suit the purchaser—the first Hinckley was built for a lobsterman. And as surprising as it may seem, the elements that made the Hinckley lobster boats such a generations-long success are integral to the design of Hinckley yachts today.

Early on, Hinckley boats were wooden, as were all sail and motorboats in those days. Ever innovative, though, Hinckley designers were early adopters of fiberglass and in 1959 the company launched the Bermuda 40, a design cited as a game-changer in the boat-building business. That boat's lighter and stronger fiberglass hull and its speed (Henry Hinckley was an aeronautical engineer) established Hinckley as the builder of exceptional quality sailing yachts, a reputation the company maintains to this day.

Design, construction, craftsmanship, and performance are the hallmarks of a Hinckley. Their aesthetic beauty is as unmistakable to those who admire them from a waterfront seat at CRU as it is to an experienced sailor. Ranging in size from twenty-nine to fifty-five feet, the graceful shape and glistening brightwork of a Hinckley never fail to draw the eye. Luxurious yet sporty, the boats exemplify a truly timeless beauty, which is exactly how visitors and residents describe the island of Nantucket.

FRESH SLICED MELON

Fresh fruit for dessert sometimes doesn't seem that exciting, but when the fruit is at its peak, it's the perfect choice. And it couldn't be easier to prepare.

INGREDIENTS

1 cantaloupe (or any perfectly ripe summer melon)
1 pint raspberries
Borage flowers or fresh chamomile flowers

If preparing this dessert to take as a picnic that will be eaten on a boat, simply slice the melon in half. Remove the seeds but leave the rind in place. Cut long slices of melon and shingle them on a tray. Sprinkle with the fresh berries and blossoms. Cover with a lid or wrap tightly with plastic wrap. Keep in a cooler with ice packs.

If you will be taking this dessert to the beach, slice off each end of the melon. Rest the melon on one of the cut flat surfaces and remove the rind by running the knife down the sides of the melon, working your way around the melon until all the rind is removed. Halve the melon and remove the seeds. Dice the melon into bite-size pieces. Transfer to a container with a lid and top with the berries and blossoms. Pop it into your beach cooler.

The fruit will keep for 1 day refrigerated.

SLICED SUMMER TOMATOES WITH GREEN GODDESS DRESSING

All winter I look forward to late summer when the tomatoes from the local farms are bursting with flavor. This salad showcases not only the tomatoes but also lots of fragrant herbs in the Green Goddess dressing. Typically, I will use any variety of herbs; anything leafy and green is great but stay away from hearty herbs, such as rosemary, sage, and thyme.

FOR THE GREEN GODDESS DRESSING

½ cup fresh cilantro leaves

¼ cup fresh tarragon leaves

¼ cup fresh flat-leaf parsley leaves

⅓ cup mayonnaise

½ cup sour cream

½ ripe avocado

2 scallions

1½ teaspoons fresh lemon juice

1 garlic clove

½ teaspoon kosher salt

FOR THE SALAD

2 pounds ripe tomatoes, cored and sliced

1 pint cherry tomatoes, halved

2 scallions, thinly sliced

Nasturtium flowers, chervil, or tarragon leaves

Extra-virgin olive oil

Freshly cracked black pepper

TO MAKE THE DRESSING: Wash the herbs in a bowl of cool water and pat dry. Coarsely chop the herbs and place them in a blender. Add the mayonnaise, sour cream, avocado, scallions, lemon juice, garlic, and salt and process until pureed. Refrigerate until ready to use. (The dressing can be stored for up to 2 days in the refrigerator but may thicken a bit. If so, it can be thinned with a little buttermilk or extra lemon juice.)

TO MAKE THE SALAD: Arrange the tomatoes on a platter. Drizzle with the dressing. Garnish the salad with the sliced scallions, nasturtium flowers, and extra herbs. Finish with a light drizzle of oil and freshly cracked black pepper. Serve.

SURFCASTING AND SUNSETS

SUMMER'S END

RECIPES FOR
SURFCASTING AND SUNSETS

Grilled Littleneck Clams with
Cilantro-Lime Butter

Burrata with Fig and Olive Tapenade

Harissa Grilled Tuna with Leeks Vinaigrette

Classic Nantucket Bluefish

Summer Bean Salad with Cherry Tomatoes,
Bacon, and Cider Vinaigrette

Salt Water–Soaked Corn

Vanilla-and-Rum Grilled Plums with
Orange-Scented Pound Cake

Ah, September on Nantucket. The air is still warm and so is the water. The tomatoes and corn and green beans—all the locally grown produce—are at their peak. The crowds of summer visitors are thinning. It's a lovely time on the island but the days are getting a bit shorter. It's time to acknowledge that summer is ending and savor every last bit of the fleeting, shimmering season we anticipate with longing all year.

For some, that will mean early-morning surfcasting for bluefish and striped bass, prolific along Nantucket's shores in September. The beaches are largely empty at that time of day; you'll have the place to yourself. The sound of the surf, the soft warm air, the repetitive motions of casting—is this meditation disguised as a sport?

This is also the month when the island's farm stands resemble the plant world's version of late-summer's fireworks. Bursting with flavor, the almost overwhelming selections are as good as it gets for farm-to-table aficionados, including all of us at CRU, where our menu reflects that local bounty.

In September, even though the days are getting shorter, the sunsets seem to linger longer on the island. You can catch a spectacular view of it from virtually any site but as the air cools, it's wonderful to enjoy it from indoors.

At this time of year, the setting sun casts a light that saturates the CRU dining rooms, enchanting all who experience it. Faces glow, wine and cocktails shimmer, and the unmistakable wistful end of summer is embodied in the shifting reflections on the water just beyond the windows.

Wherever you are, you can celebrate summer's end with the recipes in this chapter and raise a glass of CRU's favorite rosé while you make plans to return to Nantucket next September, for a much longer stay.

GRILLED LITTLENECK CLAMS WITH CILANTRO-LIME BUTTER

Most restaurant workers are given Mondays or Tuesdays off from work, as they are typically the slowest days of the week. For me, those sunshine-filled days were most often spent at the beach with friends, swimming, playing games, and grilling. From those days, this is the dish that I remember most vividly. Easy to make and easy to eat with your hands. Well, one hand, as the other holds an ice-cold beer.

INGREDIENTS

1 cup (2 sticks) unsalted butter, softened
½ jalapeño, seeded and thinly sliced
2 garlic cloves, thinly sliced
24 live littleneck clams, scrubbed
1 ciabatta or baguette, sliced
  ½ inch thick
2 limes, cut in half
¼ cup chopped fresh cilantro leaves and stems

Preheat the grill to medium-high heat.

Combine the butter, jalapeño, and garlic in a medium stainless-steel bowl.

Place the littlenecks on the grill. Set the bowl with the sauce ingredients next to the clams on the grill and cook until the garlic begins to caramelize and soften. When the clams begin to open, immediately transfer them to the bowl. Monitor the heat in the bowl: if the butter gets too hot, remove the bowl from the grill or place it on a cooler area of the grill.

As space allows, begin grilling the bread slices, turning once until each side is a light golden brown; transfer to a platter.

When the clams are done, squeeze the lime halves into the bowl with the clams and butter mixture, and add the chopped cilantro. Toss quickly and serve the bowl of clams family-style alongside the grilled bread.

BURRATA WITH FIG AND OLIVE TAPENADE

→ SERVES 6 ←

Figs and olives are a great match for one another. They are always my go-to accompaniments for a cheese course at the end of a wine dinner. Whether I knead them both into a bread dough for toast, serve them whole on the side, or puree them together for this flavorsome tapenade, they combine to a perfect balance of savory and sweet.

The burrata we serve at CRU is made locally by my friend Elizabeth. Her Nantucket company, Gioa, makes the creamiest stracciatella, burrata, and fresh mozzarella you can imagine. The cheeses can be purchased at a few local farms around the island. They are definitely worth seeking out to serve with sliced summer tomatoes or, as we do at CRU, with local greens and this fig and olive tapenade.

Dried figs can easily be substituted for the fresh. If using dried figs, let all the ingredients sit together for an hour to soften the figs before pulsing in a food processor.

FOR THE TAPENADE

8 garlic cloves

¼ cup olive oil

6 fresh figs, stemmed and halved

½ cup pitted dry-cured black olives

½ cup pitted kalamata olives

1 orange, zested

1 teaspoon chopped fresh rosemary

1 teaspoon coriander seeds, toasted and lightly crushed

FOR THE BURRATA

6 small burrata

6 cups loosely packed arugula or mizuna greens

¼ cup green or opal basil leaves

2 tablespoons fresh lemon juice

4 tablespoons extra-virgin olive oil

TO MAKE THE TAPENADE: In a small saucepan, cook the garlic in the oil over very low heat until the garlic becomes soft, 15 to 20 minutes. Remove from the heat and transfer the

(continued)

garlic to a food processor; reserve the oil. Add the figs, olives, orange zest, rosemary, and coriander and pulse until the mixture is still a bit chunky. Drizzle in the roasted garlic oil as the processor is running. Transfer to a bowl, cover, and chill the tapenade until ready to serve.

TO PREPARE THE BURRATA: Spread the tapenade on a platter or divide among 6 plates. Place the burrata on top of the tapenade. Toss the arugula and basil with the lemon juice and oil, then arrange the greens over the burrata and serve.

NANTUCKET'S WHALING MUSEUM

Cited by travel writer Andrew Harper as "one of the ten best places to see in America before you die," Nantucket's Whaling Museum offers unparalleled insights into the island's past. If you're wondering how important that history could be—after all, Nantucket is a small island, thirty miles from the mainland—you may be surprised to learn that Nantucket was, for a time, one of the world's major centers of commerce. During the late nineteenth and early twentieth centuries, Nantucket was the whaling capital of the world, a status that made it one of the wealthiest communities in America. Whale oil was one of the most valuable commodities on the globe: when adjusted for inflation, a single gallon of the oil fetched the equivalent of fifty dollars and an ounce of ambergris more than a thousand dollars.

Still, should the museum's name conjure up images of a dim, lifeless place you would just as soon skip (perhaps you're picturing a dusty stuffed whale?), think again. Housed in a spacious and handsome brick building dating back to 1847 and now seamlessly connected to a newer (1971) structure with soaring ceilings and huge rooms flooded with natural light, the museum is anything but stodgy. Instead, you'll find eleven world-class galleries housing carefully curated permanent multimedia collections as well as changing exhibits—all showcasing the dangers and rewards of the now long-gone whaling business as well as daily life during that era.

The past comes to life within these rooms through images, artifacts, and archival films of whaling including a gripping black-and-white reel of an authentic "Nantucket sleigh ride." The hauntingly poignant skeleton of a forty-six-foot-long sperm whale; the tale of the whaleship *Essex* (inspiration for Herman Melville's *Moby-Dick*), told aloud; Ric Burns's evocative documentary *Nantucket*; the Discovery Room for children—all these gems and more are why you'll likely be surprised when you notice how much time has passed since you entered the museum.

Don't miss Tucker's Rooftop, the deck atop the museum (accessible by circular staircase or elevator), where you can take in an unobstructed panoramic view of Nantucket Harbor—stunning any time of year. Be sure to check out their summer calendar for events featuring DJs, live music, and cocktail soirees on the rooftop.

It's no wonder that Nantucket's Whaling Museum is accredited by the American Association of Museums, an honor bestowed upon fewer than one of every twenty-two museums in the United States.

HARISSA GRILLED TUNA WITH LEEKS VINAIGRETTE

→ SERVES 6 ←

Leeks vinaigrette was often part of our staff meals in France. It was a dish I had never seen before. The leeks were boiled until meltingly tender and then simply dressed with vinegar and olive oil. At CRU, we marinate the leeks in a saffron vinaigrette and use them in any dish that needs both acidity and a dose of nostalgia for the South of France.

The vinaigrette can be made up to two days ahead of time and kept in the refrigerator.

Be sure to make the harissa a day or more before you plan to make this recipe. Or, you can purchase it at any good market, if you prefer.

FOR THE LEEKS VINAIGRETTE

Kosher salt

3 leeks, white and light green
    parts only, sliced and washed

½ teaspoon coriander seeds

½ teaspoon fennel seeds

¼ teaspoon saffron

½ cup white wine vinegar

½ cup olive oil

1½ tablespoons honey

1 teaspoon fresh thyme leaves

½ teaspoon salt

FOR THE TUNA

1½ pounds tuna, cut into
    6 steaks

¼ cup Harissa (page 189)

¼ cup kalamata olives, halved
    and pitted

TO MAKE THE LEEKS VINAIGRETTE: Bring 4 quarts of salted water to a boil in a large pot. Drop the leeks into the boiling water and cook for 3 minutes or until they are completely tender. Rinse the leeks in cold water to stop the cooking and then drain them completely.

(continued)

In a small skillet, lightly toast the coriander and fennel seeds over medium-high heat. When you begin to smell the spices, add the saffron and toast for 30 more seconds. Transfer to a mortar and pestle and lightly crush the spices.

Transfer the crushed spices to a bowl and add the vinegar, oil, honey, thyme, and salt. Then add the blanched leeks. Toss together lightly.

TO COOK THE TUNA: Preheat the grill to high heat.

Rub the tuna steaks with the harissa. Place the tuna on the hot grill; once you are able to move the tuna, which should take about 3 minutes, turn each piece over and cook an additional 2 minutes. Remove to a platter. Top the tuna with the leeks vinaigrette, garnish with the olives, and serve.

NOTE: The leeks vinaigrette can be made up to 2 days ahead of time and stored in a glass jar in the refrigerator. Bring to room temperature before using.

HARISSA

Harissa has been in my life for quite some time now. It was a main component of my favorite late-night bite while working in France. A half of a baguette piled with lamb merguez and French fries. The sandwich came with two sauces: my beloved mayonnaise and my new *ami*, harissa. Spiced, but not too spicy, this pepper paste from North Africa is incredibly versatile. At CRU, we mix it with mayo for our fries, with tuna for tartare, and rub it on lamb chops before they hit the grill.

INGREDIENTS

2 ancho chiles (dried whole poblano chiles)

2 roasted red peppers

5 garlic cloves

2 tablespoons olive oil

2 teaspoons sherry vinegar

1 teaspoon kosher salt

1 teaspoon smoked paprika

1 teaspoon ground cumin

1 teaspoon ground coriander

½ teaspoon crushed red pepper flakes or Aleppo pepper

⅛ teaspoon ground cinnamon

Soak the ancho chiles in water overnight at room temperature. Once they are plumped and pliable, remove their stems and seeds and place them in a blender. Add the red peppers, garlic, oil, vinegar, salt, paprika, cumin, coriander, pepper flakes, and cinnamon and puree.

The paste will keep in the refrigerator for up to 1 week. It also freezes perfectly.

CLASSIC NANTUCKET BLUEFISH

Rocco grew up eating this Nantucket classic every summer. Our favorite fisherman, Brian Borgeson, otherwise known as Boomby, the captain of Absolute Sport Fishing, also loves bluefish, especially when it's prepared like this. Boomby's play on this recipe is to ease up on the Dijon and add curry powder in its place.

The marinated bluefish is also fantastic grilled, especially at the beach. Simply omit the breadcrumb topping and bring the marinated fish to the beach in your cooler.

During the winter months, when bluefish isn't available, I substitute salmon.

INGREDIENTS

⅓ cup mayonnaise

2 tablespoons Dijon mustard

1 tablespoon fresh lemon juice, plus lemon wedges for serving

½ teaspoon kosher salt

¼ teaspoon freshly ground black pepper

2½ to 3 pounds bluefish fillets, skinned and cut into 6 portions

¾ cup panko breadcrumbs

3 tablespoons unsalted butter, melted

2 teaspoons fresh thyme leaves

1 garlic clove, minced

Lemon wedges, for serving

Mix the mayonnaise, mustard, lemon juice, ¼ teaspoon salt, and pepper well in a bowl; coat each piece of bluefish on all sides with the mixture. Arrange the fish in a 9-by-13-inch pan. Refrigerate for up to 2 hours while preparing the panko topping.

Preheat the oven to 400°F.

Mix the panko, butter, thyme, garlic, and ¼ teaspoon salt in a medium bowl. Sprinkle the mixture evenly over the pieces of bluefish.

Bake the bluefish for 15 to 20 minutes or until the coating is golden brown and the fish just begins to pull apart.

Serve immediately, with lemon wedges.

OUR FAVORITE ROSÉ FOR LATE SUMMER:
CHÂTEAU SAINTE MARGUERITE, WINEMAKER JEAN-PIERRE FAYARD

Set in Provençe on 250 acres facing the Mediterranean, the land at Château Sainte Marguerite that isn't planted with grape vines is dotted with palm trees and a grove of pines. A beautiful sanctuary for the senses, the winery has been in operation since 1929 but the ground it sits on has been cultivated for centuries. The climate and soil are considered exceptional for the production of fine wines, which is why in 1955 the winery obtained Cru Classé classification, a distinction that recognizes high standards of winemaking, quality, and adherence to the French tradition of viniculture.

Now owned and operated by Brigitte and Jean-Pierre Fayard, who acquired Château Sainte Marguerite in 1977, the estate is producing wines that are recognized around the world. They are proud of their commitment to organic agriculture and the guarantee that their wines are free of chemical additives.

Provençe is internationally acclaimed for its rosé wines—dry, refreshing, and pale-hued, these wines suit the Mediterranean cuisine of exquisite seafood, vegetables, and fruits. Dry rosé wine is a staple in the south of France but, across the entire country, rosé outsells white wine. If you've shied away from rosé wine, thinking it's sweet, you are in for a pleasant surprise. (It's true that a typical American blush wine is sugary but rosé from Provençe is not; it is, by definition, a dry wine.)

Rosé wine is made from red grapes, and its pink color comes from the amount of time the grape skins are kept in contact with the fermenting juice. Within the rosé category, though, you'll find variety; some are fuller, some lighter. In Provençe, rosé wines can encompass a range of colors, textures, and flavors.

We love the finesse, elegance, and delightful aroma of **Château Sainte Marguerite Rosé**. It is a perfect seaside-lunch wine but suited for other occasions as well. Crisp and bright and dry, it naturally goes well with the cuisine at CRU and the foods that our guests love.

SUMMER BEAN SALAD WITH CHERRY TOMATOES, BACON, AND CIDER VINAIGRETTE

→ SERVES 6 ←

This salad is so vibrant and beautiful at the height of the summer. Bright green and yellow beans, juicy cherry tomatoes, and lots of fresh herbs make this salad the highlight of any table or beach picnic. When we make this salad at CRU, we use a variety of dried or fresh beans in addition to the chickpeas—lima, fava, or butter beans are great additions, not to mention all the pretty speckled beans like the cranberry, cowboy beans, black-eyed, and yellow-eyed peas. Any combination works perfectly with this salad. Canned beans work perfectly well in this gorgeous salad.

INGREDIENTS

Kosher salt

1 pound green beans or wax beans (or a combination), trimmed

½ red onion, thinly sliced

⅓ cup apple cider vinegar

1 tablespoon whole-grain Dijon mustard

1 teaspoon honey

1½ cups cherry tomatoes, sliced in half

1 cup bacon lardons, cooked and drained

1 cup cooked chickpeas

1 cup cooked cranberry beans or red kidney beans

1 cup mixed chopped fresh herbs (such as dill, basil, and flat-leaf parsley)

⅓ cup extra-virgin olive oil

Bring a large pot of salted water to a boil. Have a bowl of ice water ready to chill the beans after they've been blanched. Add the string beans to the boiling water and cook for 3 to 5 minutes or until they are just tender. Immediately transfer them to the ice water. Once chilled, remove them from the water and set aside on towels to dry.

In a large bowl, combine the onion with the vinegar, mustard, 1 teaspoon salt, and honey. Allow the sliced onions to sit in the vinaigrette for five minutes. Then add the remaining ingredients. Toss together gently and serve.

SALT WATER–SOAKED CORN

→ SERVES 4 TO 8 ←

This recipe is so fun. My friend Katie used to make it every week at Great Point. Great Point is one of the outermost beaches on Nantucket that is only accessible by boat or over-sand vehicles. It's a really special and secluded place to spend the day, reading, surfcasting, and grilling. Just be careful the seals don't steal your lunch!

Soaking the corn in the salt water not only seasons the corn, but the water soaked up by the husks will help steam the corn from the heat of the grill. No salt necessary.

INGREDIENTS

6 to 8 ears sweet corn, in the husks

If cooking at the beach, bring 2 plastic garbage bags or 1-gallon sealable storage bags. Pull or cut the very top of the husk off each ear, leaving the rest of the husk alone. Place the corn in a plastic bag and then into another bag to help prevent any punctures. Dip the bags into the ocean, filling with sea water. Tie or seal the bag and let the corn sit in the sea water for at least 1 hour.

If cooking the corn at home, fill a kitchen sink with 1 gallon of cold water and 1 cup of kosher salt. Place the corn in the salty water for at least 1 hour before grilling.

Preheat the grill to medium-high heat. Grill the corn until the husks begin to char. Peel the corn and enjoy.

VANILLA-AND-RUM GRILLED PLUMS WITH ORANGE-SCENTED POUND CAKE

→ SERVES 8 ←

Jane is the inspiration behind this recipe, as she loves a long day at the beach filled with rosé, snacks, and lots of swimming in between. She always has quite the spread at the beach and she's even been known to grill duck with fresh plums!

This is a great "beach-friendly" dessert. Everything can be made ahead of time and transported unrefrigerated. Simply toss the plums into the rum syrup after grilling and serve with the cake.

Disclaimer . . . the rum makes this sauce boozy. It's modeled after a French baba au rhum soaking liquid. If you'd like something a bit milder, cook the sauce for a few minutes to cook off the alcohol.

FOR THE CAKE

1½ cups cake flour

¼ teaspoon baking powder

¼ teaspoon kosher salt

½ cup milk

1 teaspoon vanilla paste

1 teaspoon grated orange zest plus 2 tablespoons orange juice

¾ cup (1½ sticks) unsalted butter

1½ cups sugar

3 extra large eggs

FOR THE SYRUP AND PLUMS

½ cup sugar

½ cup water

1 vanilla bean, split lengthwise

4 tablespoons (½ stick) unsalted butter

½ cup spiced rum

6 plums or pluots, pitted and quartered

(continued)

TO MAKE THE CAKE: Preheat the oven to 350°F. Grease and flour a 9-by-5-inch loaf pan.

In a bowl, combine the flour, baking powder, and salt; set aside. In another small bowl, combine the milk, vanilla paste, and orange zest and juice; set aside.

In a mixer with the paddle attachment, cream the butter and sugar until they become extremely light and fluffy. Add the eggs one at a time and beat until completely incorporated. The mixture will be pale yellow, light and airy.

Add half of the flour mixture to the butter mixture and beat to combine, then add half of the milk mixture and beat. Repeat with the remaining flour and milk mixtures.

Pour the batter into the prepared pan and bake for 50 to 60 minutes, or until a cake tester inserted in the center comes out clean. Transfer the pan to a wire rack and let cool completely before removing from the pan.

TO MAKE THE SYRUP AND PLUMS: Combine the sugar, water, and vanilla bean in a small saucepan over medium-high heat. Bring to a boil and reduce to a simmer; add the butter and cook for 2 minutes. Remove the pan from the heat and add the rum. (This sauce can be stored at room temperature for a day or two before using.)

Preheat the grill to medium-high heat. Grill the plums for 8 minutes until slightly softened and charred on the edges. In a bowl, toss the warm grilled plums with the rum syrup. (You can achieve a similar effect with the plums under a broiler if you prefer. Watch closely so they do not burn.)

Slice the cake and top each portion with plums and rum syrup. Serve immediately.

NANTUCKET BAY SCALLOPS

THE ISLAND'S MOST DELICIOUS DELICACY

There are many varieties of scallops but none as sought-after around the world as Nantucket bay scallops. Although they're sold as a high-priced delicacy in gourmet markets from New York to San Francisco, there is, needless to say, no better place to enjoy them than on Nantucket—and there is no better place to have them than at CRU Oyster Bar Nantucket.

The commercial season for harvesting Nantucket bay scallops begins the first day of November and runs through the end of March. The month of October is reserved for Nantucket's longstanding tradition of non-commercial harvesting of bay scallops—called "family scalloping." Even though family scalloping is considered recreational, a license is required and there is a catch limit.

An integral part of Nantucket's heritage, the commercial bay scallop fishery has provided an important livelihood for generations of islanders. And it appears that tradition will continue: shellfish biologists' research shows that the waters off Nantucket support a viable bay scallop population. The limited season for harvesting them and the strict regulations on catch volume, shell size, and how they are gathered means the Nantucket habitat can continue to support the world's oldest continually sustained wild bay scallop fishery.

For fans of CRU's cuisine, that's good news, indeed.

Since the delicate yet rich flavor of a Nantucket bay scallop is best enjoyed without a lot of fuss, this chapter gives you just two recipes—an exquisite way to serve them raw and a pasta dish where the scallops are sautéed and enhanced with a champagne butter sauce. Enjoy!

RECIPES FOR

NANTUCKET
BAY SCALLOPS

Crudo of Nantucket Bay Scallops
with Ginger Mignonette and Pear

Nantucket Bay Scallops with
Fresh Pasta and Champagne Butter

CRUDO OF NANTUCKET BAY SCALLOPS WITH GINGER MIGNONETTE AND PEAR

→ SERVES 4 AS A MAIN COURSE OR 6 AS A FIRST COURSE ←

This simple crudo is a stunner: perfect around the holidays and very easy to prepare ahead of time. If white soy sauce is not available, do not substitute regular soy sauce. Instead, substitute a sprinkle of good flake sea salt, after the garnishes are added, just before serving. At CRU, we love to use Maldon salt or Fleur de Sel.

FOR THE VINAIGRETTE

1 small shallot, finely minced

2 tablespoons white soy sauce

1 tablespoon rice wine vinegar

1 tablespoon honey

1 teaspoon finely grated fresh ginger

FOR THE CRUDO

1 pound Nantucket bay scallops, cleaned

½ pear, cored and sliced lengthwise into thin pieces

2 tablespoons pomegranate seeds

1 tablespoon extra-virgin olive oil

Coarsely chopped celery leaves (light green only)

TO MAKE THE VINAIGRETTE: Whisk together the shallot, soy sauce, vinegar, honey, and ginger. (This may be done up to a day in advance; transfer the vinaigrette to a glass jar with a tight-fitting lid and store in the refrigerator.)

TO MAKE THE CRUDO: Place the scallops, pear, pomegranate seeds, oil, and celery leaves in a large bowl. Add the vinaigrette and toss gently to combine. Serve immediately on chilled plates.

NANTUCKET BAY SCALLOPS WITH FRESH PASTA AND CHAMPAGNE BUTTER

» SERVES 6 «

This is the first dish I can remember that made me want to become a chef. Dinner at my grandparents' country club was always a special treat, as we typically never went out to restaurants as a family. The club's dining room gave me my first experience of having not only scallops but also fresh pasta and a classic beurre blanc. I wanted to know how all of it was made. My grandmother informed ten-year-old me that I should go to culinary school to learn such things. So that was that.

We make this luxurious dish at CRU every Christmas Stroll Weekend at the height of Nantucket bay scallop season. Regular sea scallops can be used as well in this dish. Simply allow a little more time for searing them.

INGREDIENTS

Kosher salt

2 shallots, minced

½ bottle champagne or sparkling wine (nothing sweet)

½ cup (1 stick) unsalted butter, room temperature

1 pound fresh pasta, such as tagliatelle

1 tablespoon vegetable oil

2 pounds Nantucket bay scallops, cleaned and patted dry

Garnishes such as minced fresh chives or chervil, shaved truffles, or caviar

Bring a large pot of salted water to a boil.

Meanwhile, in a medium saucepan, combine the shallots and champagne over medium-high heat. Cook until there is only ¼ inch of liquid left in the pan. Reduce the heat to the lowest setting and whisk in the butter 1 tablespoon at a time until completely incorporated. Remove from the heat and season with 2 teaspoons salt.

Add the pasta to the boiling water and cook until al dente.

While the pasta is cooking, heat a large skillet over high heat.

(continued)

Drain the pasta, reserving ½ cup of the pasta water, and return it to the pot. Add the butter sauce and cover to keep warm.

Add the oil to the preheated skillet. Season the scallops with a pinch of salt. Remove the pan from the heat and add the scallops in an even layer. Return the pan to the heat and do not touch the scallops for 3 minutes, keeping the heat on high. Check 1 scallop to make sure it is brown on the bottom. If so, give the pan a quick shake to roll the scallops over a few times and immediately add the seared scallops to the pasta.

Lightly toss together the scallops, pasta, and sauce. Top with any of the garnish options and serve immediately.

OUR WINE AND CHAMPAGNE PICKS FOR NANTUCKET BAY SCALLOPS

To accompany Crudo of Nantucket Bay Scallops, we recommend **Christian Moreau Chablis Vaillons Premier Cru.** The soil on the left bank of the Serein River, the location of the Christian Moreau vineyards, is rich in the fossilized shells of small oysters. This terroir gives the wine a fresh and lively minerality with nice acidity. Its notes of citrus, white flowers, and nectarines are a perfect pairing with our fresh Nantucket bay scallops.

The perfect accompaniment to Nantucket Bay Scallops with Fresh Pasta and Champagne Butter is **Pol Roger Vintage Champagne.** Its composition of 60 percent Pinot Noir grapes and 40 percent Chardonnay grapes creates aromas of white fruit and brioche. This sophisticated champagne from Epernay, France, is full-bodied with creamy structure that complements this dish's buttery richness.

HOW TO SHUCK A SCALLOP; HOW TO STORE FRESH SCALLOPS BEFORE COOKING

If you're going to shuck (open) fresh live scallops yourself, the first step is purchasing the proper knife, which you can find at culinary supply stores.

The blade is short (usually two inches long) and blunt-tipped, and often curved so that it can slide cleanly under the scallop meat where it is attached to the shell.

Wearing a protective glove, hold the scallop in the palm of your hand with the darker shell facing up. Insert the tip of the knife as close to the hinge as possible; give it a little twist. When you feel the tension release, flip off the top shell. Using the tip of the knife, lift off the loose substance that surrounds the scallop meat, and discard it. Pressing the knife's blade against the shell, move it under the scallop, and drop it into a chilled glass bowl. Work as quickly as you can and as soon as you're done, cover the bowl and refrigerate it.

Fresh scallops should always be stored in a covered glass container in the refrigerator. If you purchase shucked scallops in a plastic container, transfer them to glass as soon as you get home. Scallops stored in plastic will not stay fresh as long as those stored in glass, and they can develop an unpleasant coating of slime. Cover the glass bowl so the scallop meat stays moist and flavorful. They should be used within twenty-four hours if you are having them in a crudo preparation, or within three days if the dish will be cooked. The sooner you use them, the more flavorful they will be.

FALL FOR NANTUCKET

THE ROMANCE OF THE FADING LIGHT AND FLEETING DAYS

RECIPES FOR
FALL
FOR NANTUCKET

Gougères

Clams Stuffed with Bacon and Herbed
Breadcrumbs

Lobster Bisque

Roast Chicken with Lemon and Garlic Jus

Warm Farro Salad with Walnuts and Kale

Delicata Squash with Feta, Mint,
and Pomegranate

Spiced Cranberry Jam

Pear Tarte Tatin with Nutmeg
Crème Fraîche

October on the island holds its own appeal. It's the one month of the year allocated for recreational scalloping (commercial harvesting of Nantucket bay scallops begins November 1), and it's the month the leaves begin to turn, lending an entirely different look to historic downtown as well as to the roads that lead out to the ends of the island. The hard squashes—butternut, Hubbard, acorn, and pumpkins—are ready to be picked at the local farms, complementing meals that call for richer wines and heavier beers. Entertaining moves indoors. It's the perfect time for cozying up as the days get shorter and the light gets softer.

October is also the month of Nantucket's cranberry harvest and festival. Cranberries, grown on Nantucket since 1857, were an important part of the local economy until the 1940s. Now, the Nantucket Conservation Foundation owns the last two remaining bogs under cultivation: Milestone Bog (195 acres and one of the oldest continually operated farms on Nantucket) and Windswept Bog (thirty-seven acres and one of the few certified organic cranberry bogs in the United States). Combined, the two sites produce nearly two million pounds of cranberries a year.

If you're looking for an activity to anchor your stay, plan your visit to include the second weekend in October when the Nantucket Conservation Foundation hosts the annual Cranberry Festival. You can see how cranberries are farmed and harvested and tour the bogs, where two cranberry experts answer questions and share interesting facts about cranberry farming. There's live music and a petting "zoo" of goats and other animals (always a hit with young children). There's a barbecue and lots of opportunities for participating in activities. Or you can simply enjoy the spectacular autumn scenery.

Whether or not you visit during the Cranberry Festival, you'll find October to be a wonderful month on Nantucket: the island is noticeably less crowded, it's easier to get restaurant reservations, and all the shops are still open. Beach strolling is still fun (it just calls for a sweater and jacket now), and it's an excellent month to take advantage of Nantucket's miles and miles of bicycle paths and hiking trails.

Fall on Nantucket is a welcome season at CRU; Chef Erin enjoys changing the menu to satisfy cool-weather appetites and highlight the best flavors of the season. It is also the month CRU guests savor the last two weeks of our summer season, although the restaurant does reopen in December for the annual Nantucket Christmas Stroll (see the next chapter for more information).

The recipes in this chapter are fall favorites at CRU and we think they will be for your own guests as well.

GOUGÈRES

The first time I visited Burgundy with Jane and Carlos, it seemed that everywhere we ate the meal began with a few gougères. Warm out of the oven, overflowing with alpine cheeses, they were the perfect small bite with a glass of Chablis or champagne. Pipe these little beauties ahead of time and pop them into the oven just as your guests are arriving—and don't forget to chill the wine.

INGREDIENTS

1 cup water

½ cup (1 stick) butter

1 cup all-purpose flour

4 extra large eggs

4 ounces Gruyère cheese, grated (1 cup)

1 ounce Parmesan cheese (½ cup)

1 tablespoon fresh thyme leaves, pulled from the stem

2 teaspoons kosher salt

1 teaspoon whole-grain Dijon mustard

½ teaspoon freshly ground black pepper

Preheat the oven to 400°F.

In a small saucepan, bring the water and butter to a boil. Add the flour and cook over medium heat, stirring constantly with a wooden spoon until the dough is smooth and pulls away from the sides of the pan. Allow to cool completely.

Beat the eggs one at a time into the cooled flour mixture, making sure each is completely incorporated before adding another. Set aside 1 tablespoon each of the Gruyère and Parmesan, then beat in the remaining Gruyère and Parmesan, the thyme, salt, mustard, and pepper.

Transfer the dough to a pastry bag fitted with a ½-inch round tip (or a 1-gallon sealable storage bag with a ½-inch hole cut in one corner) and pipe tablespoon-size mounds onto a parchment paper–lined baking sheet. Or use a 1-ounce scoop to form the gougères. Sprinkle with the reserved cheeses.

Bake for 20 minutes, until puffed and golden. Serve immediately.

CLAMS STUFFED WITH BACON AND HERBED BREADCRUMBS

This is classic New England comfort food at its best. We made a mountain of these for a Nantucket Food Pantry benefit one autumn evening. We were out of clams in thirty minutes! No one could resist these gems with their crispy tops and pillowy interior. Adding freshly shucked oysters turns this recipe into the best oyster dressing for Thanksgiving!

INGREDIENTS

1½ cups chopped bacon

½ cup chopped red onion

½ cup chopped celery

5 garlic cloves, chopped

1 teaspoon coarsely chopped fresh rosemary

1 teaspoon fresh thyme leaves

2 cups fresh untoasted breadcrumbs

¼ cup chopped fresh flat-leaf parsley

2 dozen live littleneck or cherrystone clams, scrubbed

½ cup white wine

1 lemon, cut into wedges

Preheat the oven to 400°F.

In a large cast-iron skillet, cook the bacon over medium-high heat until crispy. (Do not drain the fat from the pan.) Add the onion, celery, garlic, rosemary, and thyme and cook for 5 minutes, leaving the vegetables with a little crunch. Pour the bacon and vegetable mixture into a bowl and add the breadcrumbs and chopped parsley. Mix together quickly and set aside.

Place the clams and white wine in a large saucepan, cover, and steam over high heat until the clams are open. Once cool enough to handle, remove the clams from the shells and coarsely chop the meat; reserve the shells. Strain the cooking liquid through a fine-mesh sieve lined with cheesecloth or a clean kitchen towel.

Add the chopped clams and 1 cup of the clam cooking liquid to the stuffing. Toss to combine evenly. Arrange 36 shells on a baking sheet and divide the stuffing evenly among them. Bake for 15 minutes or until the tops become crispy. Serve immediately with the lemon wedges.

LOBSTER BISQUE

We knew when writing the menu for CRU that we would have lots and lots of lobster shells at our disposal on a daily basis. Lobster bisque is the perfect solution to such a problem. This bisque is rich and velvety with hints of orange peel, anise, and just the right amount of heat from the pepper flakes. If Pernod is unavailable, sherry or white wine would be delicious additions to this decadent soup.

INGREDIENTS

2 (1½-pound) lobsters

2 tablespoons olive oil

1 carrot, peeled and roughly chopped

1 leek, cut into 2-inch pieces and cleaned

6 garlic cloves, peeled

3 bay leaves

1 (3-ounce) can tomato paste

½ teaspoon fennel seeds

½ teaspoon coriander seeds

¼ cup Pernod

¼ cup brandy

4 cups half-and-half

4 cups heavy cream

Zest of 1 orange (removed in strips with a vegetable peeler)

4 sprigs fresh tarragon

2 teaspoons kosher salt

¼ teaspoon crushed red pepper flakes

¼ cup white rice

Fill a large stockpot halfway with water and bring to a boil. Add the lobsters, cover with the lid, return the water to a boil, and then turn off the heat. Keep the lobsters covered for 30 minutes.

After 30 minutes, remove the lobsters from the pot and let them cool on a baking sheet. Once cool enough to handle, remove the lobster meat from the shells. Set the lobster meat aside.

Heat the empty stockpot again over medium-high heat. Add the oil and the lobster shells. Cook for a few minutes to toast the shells. Add the carrot, leek, garlic, and bay leaves. Cook until the edges of the vegetables just begin to brown. Add the tomato paste, fennel seeds, and coriander seeds and cook, stirring often to coat the lobster

(continued)

shells and vegetables in the tomato paste. Add the Pernod and brandy and cook for 1 to 2 minutes to cook off the alcohol.

Add the half-and-half, cream, orange peel, tarragon sprigs, salt, and red pepper flakes. Lower the heat and simmer for 20 minutes. Add the rice and cook, stirring often, for an additional 15 minutes or until the bisque begins to thicken slightly.

While the bisque is cooking, run the lobster meat under cool running water to remove any protein or small pieces of shell. Cut the lobster into bite-size pieces and keep meat covered in the refrigerator until ready to use. (This can be done up to a day in advance.)

Strain the bisque through a fine-mesh sieve, pressing on the solids to capture as much bisque as possible. Return the strained bisque to a clean pot and add the lobster meat. Warm gently over low heat until hot. Serve immediately in prewarmed soup plates or bowls.

ROAST CHICKEN WITH LEMON AND GARLIC JUS

When I worked on the northern coast of France, my Sundays were spent walking through the local outdoor market. For dinner, I would always leave with a perfectly roasted rotisserie chicken. I admit that I had a "little crush" on the Moroccan man making those delicious chickens (was I infatuated with him or the chicken . . .). The chicken was ever so slightly kissed with North African spices and I was hooked.

This recipe is my memory's account of that blend of spices. It must be pretty good, as we certainly go through quite a bit of this spice mix on our pan-roasted chicken at CRU every summer.

INGREDIENTS

¼ teaspoon coriander seeds

¼ teaspoon fennel seeds

2 tablespoons olive oil

4 sprigs fresh thyme, picked

2 teaspoons kosher salt

¼ teaspoon freshly ground black pepper

⅛ teaspoon ground cinnamon

⅛ teaspoon ground cumin

⅛ teaspoon smoked paprika

1 (5-pound) roasting chicken, rinsed and patted dry

1 head garlic

2 cups chicken stock

3 tablespoons fresh lemon juice

With a mortar and pestle, lightly crush the coriander and fennel seeds. Transfer to a bowl and add the oil, thyme, salt, pepper, cinnamon, cumin, and paprika.

Rub the spice mixture over the chicken. Place the chicken in a roasting pan or large cast-iron skillet, tucking the wing tips under the body of the chicken. Cut the top ½ inch off

(continued)

the head of garlic and place in the pan with the chicken; let sit at room temperature for an hour. Preheat the oven to 375°F.

Roast the chicken for 1 hour and 30 minutes. The skin will slightly puff and become crispy and the legs will be easily moved. Transfer the chicken to a cutting board to rest for at least 10 minutes.

Skim off some of the fat from the pan. Squeeze the roasted garlic into the pan juices and add the chicken stock. Cook over medium-high heat to reduce the sauce to almost 1 cup. Add the lemon juice, taste, and season with salt as needed. Carve the chicken and serve with the garlicky pan sauce.

WARM FARRO SALAD WITH WALNUTS AND KALE

We are fans of grains and farro is definitely a recurring character in the CRU menu. We often serve it with our chicken or a lamb special. Different varieties of kale can be found at nearly every farm on Nantucket, and all are hearty and delicious.

This salad is absolutely perfect as is, but it is also ready for any embellishment you can throw at it—goat cheese, chickpeas, roasted beets, or a drizzle of walnut oil. This salad can handle it!

INGREDIENTS

1 cup farro

Kosher salt

1 shallot, thinly sliced

2 tablespoons sherry vinegar

1½ tablespoons fresh lemon juice

1 tablespoon honey

1 teaspoon Dijon mustard

¼ cup olive oil

1 bunch kale (Tuscan, curly, or Russian), ribs removed, leaves thinly sliced

½ cup walnuts, toasted

½ cup golden raisins

Bring 2 quarts water to a boil in a large saucepan. Add the farro and a pinch of salt and cook for 10 to 15 minutes, until tender yet still slightly chewy. Strain and let cool to room temperature.

Combine the shallot, vinegar, lemon juice, honey, and mustard in a large bowl and slowly whisk in the oil. Add the cooked farro, kale, walnuts, and raisins. Season with salt, toss to combine, and serve.

(The salad can be left at room temperature for up to an hour before serving.)

DELICATA SQUASH WITH FETA, MINT, AND POMEGRANATE

→ SERVES 6 ←

This is a great side dish, as it hits lots of notes. The squash is sweet and creamy, the feta salty and briny, and the pomegranate seeds give tartness and texture. Mint is always a great last-minute addition as it adds vibrant freshness to brighten any dish.

Cutting the squash a bit smaller and tossing all of the ingredients together turns this composed side dish into a perfect mezze dip for flatbreads.

Delicata season seems to end quite quickly in Nantucket. If you are unable to find delicata squash, butternut squash will be perfect in its place.

INGREDIENTS

6 tablespoons unsalted butter

½ stick cinnamon

6 fresh sage leaves

3½ to 4 pounds delicata squash, trimmed, seeded, and sliced into ¾-inch-thick rings

½ teaspoon kosher salt

2 ounces feta cheese, crumbled (½ cup)

½ cup pomegranate seeds

½ cup fresh mint leaves, torn

Aleppo pepper

Preheat the oven to 375°F.

Cook the butter with the cinnamon stick in a small saucepan over medium heat. Once the butter begins to smell like caramel and is beginning to brown, remove the pan from the heat and carefully add the sage leaves. Remove and discard the cinnamon stick.

Place the squash in a large bowl, add the sage brown butter and salt, and toss to coat. Arrange the squash on a baking sheet in an even layer. Bake for 15 to 20 minutes, until easily pierced with a paring knife.

Arrange the squash on a serving platter. Crumble the feta over the squash, followed by the pomegranate seeds, torn mint leaves, and Aleppo pepper. Serve immediately.

SPICED CRANBERRY JAM

When cranberries are in season, I always keep this sauce handy in my fridge. I throw a spoonful into an apple pie filling or put it on every turkey sandwich I make. The warm spices used in this recipe are redolent of the holidays.

INGREDIENTS

4 cups cranberries
1 cup brown sugar
1 cup granulated sugar
1 orange, peels and juice
1 teaspoon ground cinnamon
1/2 teaspoon ground allspice

Rinse the cranberries and remove any stems. With a vegetable peeler, make small shards of orange peel. Try to avoid getting too much of the white pith.

In a medium saucepan, combine all of the ingredients. Cook over medium-high heat until the cranberries begin to pop and break down and the sauce starts to thicken, stirring frequently. This should take about 8-10 minutes.

Keep refrigerated for up to 1 week.

Can a superlative French wine be produced by an American winemaker? Yes. Alex Gambal, American born and raised, took his family to France for an extended visit in 1993 and never left. Now, twenty-plus years later, his wines are rated among the great wines from the Burgundy region of France.

He did not intend to leave his thriving real estate business in Washington, DC. He simply wanted to experience Burgundy's wine, food, culture, and traditions. A chance introduction to an American wine broker who encouraged him to stay was the catalyst that set his life's trajectory on a new course. He spent a year studying winemaking and viniculture in Beaunne and in 1997 decided to take the leap.

At first, he started his winemaking business by purchasing wine and grapes from other growers. Eventually, he bought land and now has more than thirty acres of vineyards, which are cultivated organically. While two-thirds of his wines' grapes come from his land, he still buys grapes from top growers and, because of that, Maison Alex Gambal is able to produce about 60,000 bottles per year.

His wines are described by aficionados as "exciting, original, and stylish" as well as "models of restraint," and his **Grand Cru Charmes-Chambertin** is considered beautifully "structured and age-worthy." For Gambal, a relative newcomer in a region dominated by winemakers that span generations, these compliments are humbling. As he likes to say, "I was lucky . . . Burgundy chose me."

Alex Gambal's **Chambolle-Musigny Premier Cru "Les Charmes"** is one of our favorite wines produced by this domaine. Its floral and delicate style with cherry, plum, and silky tannins work wonders with Chef Zircher's duck confit or chicken liver mousse.

Perhaps he has been lucky, but because he models his winemaking on Burgundy's traditions, we say that his good fortune is the result of hard work and opportunity. With a personal motto of Always Do Better, Alex Gambal will, no doubt, continue to enchant us with stunning wines.

PEAR TARTE TATIN WITH NUTMEG CRÈME FRAÎCHE

While I was working in France, I made this dessert every single day. Sometimes twice a day if lunch service was really busy.

This pastry is simple and can be whipped up with very little notice as long as there is puff pastry in the freezer.

We prefer Bartlett pears for this tart, but any pear or apple will work wonderfully.

INGREDIENTS

2 sheets frozen puff pastry (one 17.3-ounce package), thawed
2 tablespoons butter, plus extra as needed
5 pears, peeled, quartered lengthwise, and cored
½ cup sugar
8 ounces crème fraîche
1 teaspoon grated fresh ginger
½ teaspoon grated nutmeg

Preheat the oven to 350°F.

Unfold the puff pastry and place one sheet on a lightly floured countertop. Place the second sheet of pastry over the first at an opposite angle. Roll the sheets lightly together with a rolling pin and set the puff pastry aside.

Heat a 12-inch cast-iron pan or ovenproof skillet over low heat. Add the butter. Once the butter is melted, arrange the pears cut side up around the pan in a decorative pattern. Sprinkle evenly with the sugar. Raise the heat to medium-high and

(continued)

cook until the sugar and pear juices caramelize. Watch the pan closely, and if an area becomes too dark too quickly, add an additional dab of cool butter to slow the caramel in that particular spot.

Once the sugar and the pear juices start to turn into a beautiful amber caramel, remove the skillet from the heat. Place the pastry over the pears and, using a butter knife, tuck the edges down around the pears. Do not use your fingers, as the caramel is very hot.

Bake for 20 to 25 minutes or until the pastry is puffed and golden. Transfer to a wire rack and let the tart rest for 5 minutes. Place a large plate on the top of the pan and, using oven mitts, carefully invert the pan. Lift the pan, leaving the tart on the plate.

In a mixing bowl, combine the crème fraîche with the grated ginger and nutmeg. Whisk until the crème fraîche is light with soft peaks.

Cut the tart into wedges and serve with the spiced crème fraîche.

A CHRISTMAS STROLL

A FESTIVE NANTUCKET TRADITION

The first weekend in December is a delightful time to be on Nantucket. That's when the island hosts its annual downtown Christmas Stroll and takes on the look of a Norman Rockwell painting come to life. The handsome brick and granite buildings in historic downtown are decorated with evergreen roping, swags, and wreaths, their tall windows sparkling with lights as shopkeepers set out elegant spreads of wine, fruitcake, holiday cookies, mulled cider, and hot chocolate to welcome shoppers.

The tradition of the stroll began forty years ago as part of the Chamber of Commerce's month-long celebration, Nantucket Noel, and has steadily grown in popularity; today, the Christmas Stroll is an internationally renowned holiday event. The joy of giving (to family, friends—and oneself!) is fully evident as shoppers spend on lavish items in world-class shops for one-of-a-kind artisan pieces for the home, or on apparel, jewelry, books, art, and other spectacular items.

Preparations for the Christmas Stroll begin weeks earlier; the day after Thanksgiving volunteers line the downtown streets with hundreds of seven-foot Christmas trees packed with decorations. Then, during a caroling ceremony at dusk, the trees are illuminated to the oohs and aahs of small children (and their taller friends). It's a magical sight no matter your age or how many times you've been present for it.

At the top of Main Street, a twenty-foot Christmas tree—visible from blocks away thanks to the elevation—is the holiday season's landmark for visitors.

Dozens of beloved traditions and festivities make the Christmas Stroll weekend truly special. On Saturday, carolers in costume sing holiday tunes at locations throughout downtown. Main Street, which is closed to automobile traffic for the day, is the site of artisan crafts' shows, holiday-themed performances, and artists' exhibitions. Midday on Saturday, the Nantucket Town Crier, dressed in full regalia, rings his bell and leads everyone to the wharves to meet Santa and Mrs. Claus, who arrive via Coast Guard cutter and then head to the Jared Coffin House to meet with children.

Even the famed Nantucket Whaling Museum is transformed into a glittering winter wonderland with its Festival of Trees showcasing nearly one hundred Christmas trees, each one adorned with unique decorations by island businesses.

CRU reopens for the Christmas Stroll for four days (from the Thursday before through Sunday), beautifully decorated for the season and serving a decadent all-day brunch every day. Chef Erin unveils a special menu of holiday-inspired dishes for the weekend including CRU's favorite: Nantucket Bay Scallops. After a day of shopping, a glass of hand-selected wine or a seasonal CRU cocktail (iced or warm) is perfect for cozying up by the CRU fireplace where you can relax and ponder the rest of the treasures you need to purchase during this special annual tradition on magical Nantucket . . .

A CHRISTMAS STROLL

Buttermilk Soufflé Pancakes with
Pecan-Date Butter and Maple-Roasted
Bananas

Potato Pancake with Horseradish
Crème Fraîche

Winter Fruit Salad with Passion
Fruit Vinaigrette

Smoked Salmon Tartine

Eggs Baked with Spicy Tomato Broth,
Chorizo, and Swiss Chard

Cranberry Cinnamon Rolls

Eggnog

NANTUCKET'S AMAZING SHOPS

It might seem contradictory that a small, remote island known for its rustic natural beauty (and whose residents are proud to maintain and protect more than thirty miles of bike paths) would also be home to stores that cater to the most discerning buyers of high-end art, one-of-a-kind pieces of jewelry, artisan crafts, clothing, and home décor. Yet that contradiction is exactly what makes Nantucket so appealing and unique.

Strolling historic downtown Nantucket to shop is a wonderful way to spend an afternoon. You'll find street after street of enticing boutiques, galleries, and cafés side by side, each one welcoming you with attractive windows and entries. A good place to start is with a walk up Main Street from the waterfront, meandering the side streets as you go.

BODEGA NANTUCKET, 2 CANDLE STREET

A beautifully curated selection of home accessories, glassware, jewelry, and furniture with the perfect mix of modern and coastal. This shop is sure to provide the ideal hostess gift, addition to your new summer home, or a beach-inspired reminder to bring home to the city.

NANTUCKET LOOMS, 51 MAIN STREET

This iconic island boutique is best known for its sumptuous hand-loomed blankets and throws—most of which are created in the building's second-floor loom room—of linen, wool, or cashmere. The designs are modern yet timeless, and the colors are evocative of the ever-enchanting Nantucket landscape. These hand-woven items are the perfect complement to their selection of the work of more than 80 local artisans including ceramics, artwork, and furniture.

MILLY & GRACE, 2 WASHINGTON STREET

Named after her grandmothers, the owner, Emily Hollister, curates her collection to highlight a balance of contemporary and classic clothing perfect for island life. Feminine dresses, delicate blouses, and cashmere wraps are the cornerstone of this boutique with dashes of home accents and gifts mixed in with just the right amount of surprise.

ATLANTIC, 18 FEDERAL STREET

Longtime summer resident Colleen Darby Wurts originally started her business in a friend's 'Sconset garage. Now, her lofty, open space on Federal Street is a whimsical collection of clothing, art, antiques, and accessories to complement any home collection.

CURRENTVINTAGE, 4 EASY STREET

Owner Elisabeth English is known for her keen eye in vintage shopping including an epic hat collection of vintage Lilly Pulitzer (for women and men). As the weather turns colder, be sure to look for fur-trimmed coats, holiday sweaters, and of course, the perfect bottle of wine.

NANTUCKET BOOKWORKS, 25 BROAD STREET

This island institution is the epicenter of all that goes on in the world of books on Nantucket. Every turn you make in this cottage-like store reveals more treasure.

SAMUEL OWEN GALLERY, 46 CENTRE STREET

This contemporary art gallery is committed to exhibiting the work of emerging artists with rotating exhibits. You won't want to miss the latest pieces.

EPERNAY WINE AND SPIRITS, 1 N BEACH STREET

This wine store has an expansive collection of fine wines, champagnes, and spirits. A must-stop on your way to Step's Beach for the perfect sunset picnic or to stock up before an afternoon sail. Owners Jenny Benzie and Kirk Baker are always on-site to help you select the perfect wine for your vacation.

This list of shops and galleries is the tip of the iceberg. Come and check out Nantucket—during the Christmas Stroll or any other time of year—and see why people make this small island a shopping destination.

BUTTERMILK SOUFFLÉ PANCAKES WITH PECAN-DATE BUTTER AND MAPLE-ROASTED BANANAS

We have been serving these pancakes since we opened CRU. They are almost like eating a piece of cake for breakfast, only better. We serve one large pancake per order, slathered with the pecan-date butter and maple-roasted bananas during the cooler months. In the summertime, we top the pancake with stone fruits or fresh berries (pictured). Letting the butter brown before adding the batter creates the irresistibly crispy caramelized edges on these pancakes.

INGREDIENTS

1½ cups buttermilk

6 extra large eggs, separated

6 tablespoons butter, melted and cooled to room temperature, plus extra for cooking the pancakes

1 teaspoon vanilla paste

2 cups all-purpose flour

½ teaspoon salt

6 tablespoons sugar

Pecan-Date Butter (recipe follows)

Maple-Roasted Bananas (recipe follows)

Preheat the oven to 425°F.

In a large bowl, whisk together the buttermilk, egg yolks, melted butter, and vanilla paste. Gently mix in the flour and salt. In a mixer with the whisk attachment, whip the egg whites and sugar to almost stiff peaks, then fold into the pancake batter.

Heat 2 6-inch cast-iron skillets (or ovenproof sauté pans) over medium heat. Add 1 tablespoon of butter to each pan. Once the butter is lightly golden and smells nutty, add 8 ounces of batter. Cook on the stovetop until golden brown on the bottom, about 2 minutes. Transfer the pan to the oven and bake for 8 minutes, until the top of the pancake is set.

Keep the first two pancakes warm while you make the remaining two.

Flip each pancake onto a plate and top with the pecan-date butter, roasted bananas, and their syrup. Serve immediately.

PECAN-DATE BUTTER

INGREDIENTS

1 cup pecans

1 tablespoon packed light brown sugar

½ teaspoon ground cinnamon

½ cup Medjool dates, pitted

½ cup (1 stick) butter, softened

½ teaspoon flake sea salt

In a food processor, grind the pecans with the brown sugar and cinnamon until the pecans are the size of peas. Add the dates, butter, and salt. Pulse to combine thoroughly.

MAPLE-ROASTED BANANAS

→ MAKES 4 SERVINGS

The bananas can be made an hour ahead of time and kept at room temperature.

INGREDIENTS

3 ripe bananas, peeled and cut into long slices on the bias

½ cup maple syrup, grade B (grade A may be too delicate for this application)

¼ cup spiced rum (optional)

Preheat the broiler. In a bowl, toss the bananas with the maple syrup and the rum (if using). Lay the bananas on a baking pan; do not overlap. Broil until golden brown on the edges. (Keep an eye on the bananas as they will burn quickly.)

POTATO PANCAKE WITH HORSERADISH CRÈME FRAÎCHE

A perfectly golden potato pancake is a very special treat. We serve this one as a large rösti-style pancake, but feel free to make smaller ones on the stovetop. Serve alongside other brunch offerings such as smoked salmon or poached eggs.

INGREDIENTS

3 pounds Yukon Gold potatoes, peeled

1 white onion

¼ cup potato flour or potato starch

1 egg, beaten

1 tablespoon chopped fresh chives

1 tablespoon kosher salt

½ cup clarified butter or vegetable oil

Flake sea salt

Horseradish Crème Fraîche (page 25)

Preheat the oven to 400°F.

Using a box grater or food processor, grate the potatoes and onion. In batches, wrap the grated potatoes and onion in a clean kitchen towel; wring out the kitchen towel over the sink until you are unable to squeeze out any more liquid.

Place the dry potato mixture in a large mixing bowl. Add the potato starch, beaten egg, chives, and salt and stir to combine.

Heat a 12-inch cast-iron skillet or ovenproof nonstick skillet over medium-high heat. Add ¼ cup of the clarified butter to the hot pan and top with the potato mixture, spreading to an even thickness. Reduce the heat to medium and cook for 10 minutes; do not touch the potatoes. Transfer the skillet to the oven and bake the pancake for 15 minutes.

Remove the pan from the oven. Using oven mitts, hold a large heatproof plate over the skillet and carefully flip the pancake onto the plate. Add the remaining ¼ cup of clarified butter to the hot pan. Once the butter has melted, return the pancake to the pan, crispy side up. Place in the oven and bake for another 10 minutes.

Remove from the oven and turn the pancake out of the pan onto a serving platter. Sprinkle the top with a little flake sea salt. Cut the pancake into wedges and serve with a pot of horseradish crème fraîche on the side.

WINTER FRUIT SALAD WITH PASSION FRUIT VINAIGRETTE

→ SERVES 6 ←

A few years ago, I spent some time in the kitchen of the Hostellerie de Levernois, a beautiful Relais & Châteaux property, located outside Beaune, France. One Saturday evening, the chef had me slice a massive bowl of fruit for the following morning's breakfast. Then together we made a vinaigrette for it to soak in overnight. To my surprise the vinaigrette was loaded with white rum! The scent and flavor of the fruit juices combined with vanilla bean and rum immediately transported me from that gray autumn Sunday in Burgundy to the French West Indies. It was spectacular.

I've added fresh passion fruit to the vinaigrette, not only for its perfume but also for its sweet-tart flavor and the crunchy black seeds that add a fun pop. If you are unable to find fresh passion fruit, a little passion fruit nectar is a fine substitute.

FOR THE VINAIGRETTE

2 ripe passion fruits

1 tablespoon white rum

1 tablespoon mild honey

2 teaspoons vanilla paste or
   1 vanilla bean, split and seeds removed

FOR THE SALAD

2 ripe pears, halved, cored, and sliced

1 grapefruit, peeled and segmented

1 blood orange, peeled and segmented

2 Cara Cara oranges, peeled and segmented

2 bananas, peeled and sliced

½ cup pomegranate seeds

¼ cup mint leaves

TO MAKE THE VINAIGRETTE: Slice the passion fruits in half and use a small spoon to scoop the orange jelly (and seeds) into a small bowl. Add the rum, honey, and vanilla paste and whisk to combine.

TO MAKE THE SALAD: The evening before you will be serving the salad, combine the pears, grapefruit, oranges, and bananas in a large bowl. Add the vinaigrette and toss gently. Cover and refrigerate overnight.

The following morning, add the pomegranate seeds and mint leaves; toss and serve.

SMOKED SALMON TARTINE

This is the very first version of CRU's smoked salmon tartine. When Wayne, our photographer, was shooting it for the first time, he couldn't believe the audacity of crème fraîche, cream cheese, and avocado all jammed onto one slice of buttered toast. Each and every layer is worth it and the pickled onion totally balances out the richness. Great for brunch or a light lunch with a salad, these little open-face sandwiches are as beautiful as they are delicious.

INGREDIENTS

2 avocados

Flake sea salt and freshly ground black pepper

4 thick slices sourdough bread

Softened butter

Horseradish Crème Fraîche (page 25)

4 ounces smoked salmon, thinly sliced

Pickled Red Onions (recipe follows)

Fresh dill sprigs

Cut the avocados in half, remove the pits, and with a large spoon, scoop the avocado halves from the peels, keeping each half intact. Slice each half horizontally into 3 pieces. Sprinkle the slices of avocado with salt and pepper.

Lightly toast the sourdough bread. Spread each piece of toast lightly with butter followed by the horseradish crème fraîche. Lay 3 slices of avocado over the cream, followed by the smoked salmon. Top with a few pickled red onions and dill sprigs. Cut each piece of toast into three pieces and serve.

PICKLED RED ONIONS

INGREDIENTS

1 red onion

2 cups red wine vinegar

1 cup sugar

2 whole allspice berries

2 star anise pods

2 bay leaves

1 teaspoon kosher salt

Slice the onion into ¼-inch-thick rounds and place in a medium bowl. In a small sauce-pan, heat the vinegar with the sugar, allspice, star anise, bay leaves, and salt until it reaches a boil. Pour the hot liquid over the sliced onion, cover, and refrigerate for at least 1 hour before serving.

EGGS BAKED WITH SPICY TOMATO BROTH, CHORIZO, AND SWISS CHARD

→ SERVES 4 TO 6 ←

These baked eggs are great for when you're having friends over for brunch because the dish can be prepared ahead of time except for adding the eggs, which is done right before serving. That's our type of brunch—more time to spend with your guests and less time fussing in the kitchen. Serve some flatbread alongside for dipping. If you don't have time to make harissa, store-bought produces equally fantastic results.

INGREDIENTS

¼ cup olive oil

1 onion, chopped

1 carrot, peeled and chopped

3 garlic cloves, chopped

1 (28-ounce) can peeled plum tomatoes

2 teaspoons kosher salt

¼ cup Harissa (page 189)

1 pound ground chorizo (Portuguese or Mexican-style chorizo sausage)

1 bunch Swiss chard, thick stems removed, sliced into 2-inch ribbons

1 (15-ounce) can chickpeas, drained and rinsed

1 tablespoon fresh lemon juice

8 extra large eggs

2 scallions, sliced

¼ cup coarsely chopped fresh cilantro leaves and stems

In a large, heavy skillet, heat the oil over medium heat. Add the onion, carrot, and garlic and cook until the onion is translucent and just starting to brown on the edges. Add the canned tomatoes and their juice, 1 teaspoon of the salt, and the harissa. Lower the heat to medium-low, cover, and cook for 30 minutes, stirring occasionally. Allow the sauce to cool and then puree it in batches in the blender. (The sauce can be prepared up to 2 days in advance.)

(continued)

Preheat the oven to 425°F.

Cook the chorizo in a large skillet over medium-high heat, breaking up the meat until fully cooked. Remove the chorizo with a slotted spoon and drain on a paper towel–lined plate. Add the Swiss chard to the chorizo fat and sauté quickly over medium-high heat. Transfer the Swiss chard to a bowl and add the drained chorizo, chickpeas, lemon juice, and remaining 1 teaspoon salt; toss to combine.

Pour the sauce into a 9-by-13-inch baking pan or gratin dish. Evenly sprinkle the chorizo mixture over the sauce. Cover with foil and bake for 25 to 30 minutes to heat thoroughly. Remove the baking dish from the oven, remove the foil and, with the back of a spoon, make eight indentations where the eggs will sit. Quickly break an egg into each of the indentations and return the pan to the oven. Bake, uncovered, for 10 minutes or until the eggs are just set. Garnish with the scallions and cilantro and serve.

CRANBERRY CINNAMON ROLLS

→ MAKES 10 CINNAMON ROLLS ←

I absolutely love cinnamon rolls. Ever since I was a young girl, I have been trying to improve my cinnamon roll game, sometimes adding caramelized apples, sometimes raisins, or a variety of nuts. But, since living on Nantucket, the cranberries are my new favorite addition. The spiced cranberry jam adds layers of warm spices and candied orange peel to the rolls, making them perfect for holiday mornings.

INGREDIENTS

1 tablespoon active dry yeast
1 cup water, room temperature
¾ cup sugar
1 egg
3½ cups all-purpose flour
1 teaspoon table salt
4 tablespoons (½ stick) unsalted
    butter, softened, plus extra
    for the bowl

2 teaspoons ground cinnamon
¾ cup Spiced Cranberry Jam
    (page 230), plus extra for
    serving
Cream Cheese Frosting (recipe
    follows)

In the bowl of a mixer fitted with the dough hook, dissolve the yeast in the water. Mix in ¼ cup of the sugar and the egg, then the flour and salt. Knead on low speed until thoroughly combined. Increase the speed to medium and add 2 tablespoons of the butter, 1 tablespoon at a time. Knead for another 3 to 5 minutes to form a smooth dough.

(continued)

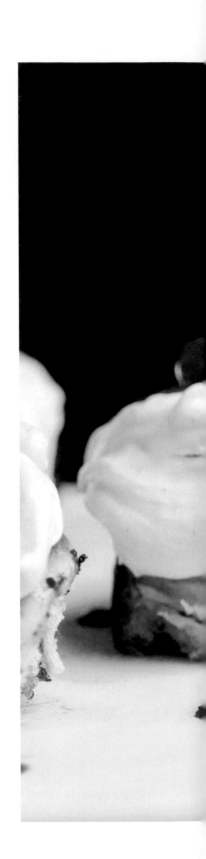

Transfer the dough to a clean, lightly buttered bowl and cover with a clean kitchen towel. Let rise until doubled in size (this will take 1 to 1½ hours).

Lightly butter a piece of parchment paper and set it into a 12-inch springform pan, allowing the paper to come all the way up the sides.

Turn the dough out onto a lightly floured work surface. Roll it to a 16-by-12-inch rectangle. Spread the remaining 2 tablespoons butter evenly over the dough and sprinkle the cinnamon and remaining ½ cup sugar over the butter, distributing evenly. Gently spread the spiced cranberry jam over the sugar mixture.

Roll the dough into a cylinder, starting with a long edge, pinching the seam at the end. Roll seam side down and slice the dough in half, being careful not to crush the roll (use a sharp serrated knife for this). Divide each half into 5 even pieces. Place the rolls into the prepared springform pan, spirals facing up. Cover with a clean kitchen towel and let rise for 45 minutes to 1 hour or until doubled in size.

Preheat the oven to 375°F.

Bake the cinnamon rolls for 20 to 25 minutes, or until the dough is completely cooked (you should not see any spongy sections, and a toothpick inserted in the dough only will come out clean). Transfer the pan to a wire rack and let the cinnamon rolls cool completely.

Frost liberally with cream cheese frosting and garnish with an additional drizzle of spiced cranberry jam. Serve.

CREAM CHEESE FROSTING

→→ MAKES ABOUT 1½ CUPS ←←

INGREDIENTS

6 ounces cream cheese, softened

4 tablespoons (½ stick) unsalted butter, softened

2 cups confectioners' sugar

1 teaspoon vanilla paste

½ teaspoon flake sea salt or kosher salt

Using a mixer with the whisk attachment, mix the cream cheese, butter, sugar, and vanilla paste on low speed until combined. Increase the speed to high and whip for 4 to 5 minutes or until the frosting is light and fluffy. Add the salt and whip 1 additional minute.

Use immediately or place a piece of plastic wrap directly on the surface and store at room temperature until ready to use. Can be made 2 days in advance.

EGGNOG

You either love eggnog or hate it. I'm crazy about it. This is the eggnog of my dreams. It's velvety with a frothy foam on top and lots and lots of freshly grated nutmeg. Some people prefer bourbon in their nog; I tend to have it as is, or with a little bit of good spiced rum. At CRU we love to use Twenty Boat Rum, which is made in the town of Truro on Cape Cod.

INGREDIENTS

4 cups whole milk
4 cups heavy cream
1 vanilla bean, split
2 cinnamon sticks
1 tablespoon grated nutmeg
¼ teaspoon kosher salt
4 extra large eggs, separated, plus 12 extra large egg yolks
1¼ cups sugar
Twenty Boat Rum (or rum of your choice) (optional)

Combine the milk, cream, vanilla bean, cinnamon sticks, nutmeg, and salt in a medium saucepan and cook over medium-low heat for 10 to 15 minutes.

Meanwhile, combine the egg yolks with 1 cup of the sugar in a medium bowl and whisk until they are light and fluffy. Temper the yolks by adding a ladle full of the hot milk mixture while whisking, then add the tempered yolk mixture to the saucepan and continue to cook over medium-low heat, stirring constantly, until it begins to thicken. Strain through a fine-mesh sieve and refrigerate until thoroughly chilled.

Whip the egg whites with the remaining ¼ cup sugar to soft peaks and fold them into the eggnog. (The eggnog can be refrigerated for up to 2 days until ready to serve.)

Pour into small glasses and add a splash of rum (if using) to each and serve.

ALL IS QUIET

CELEBRATING NEW YEAR'S EVE CRU-STYLE

RECIPES FOR
ALL IS QUIET

Caviar and Blinis

Roasted Oysters with Garlic and
Parsley Butter

Lobster Cocktail

Confit-Style Duck Legs

Macomber Turnip and Black Truffle Gratin

Chocolate Pots de Crème

S een from the air in late December, the snow-covered windswept island of
Nantucket, lying thirty miles out to sea, appears perfectly still and quiet. Yet
there are reasons to visit, and plenty to do for those who find this time of year on
the island particularly romantic.

It's fitting that Nantucket—an island beloved for its natural beauty and walkable
landscape—offers residents and visitors lots of outdoor activities leading up to any
extravagant plans for New Year's Eve. The Linda Loring Nature Foundation walking
trail overlooks the North Head of Long Pond, where numerous species of water-
fowl spend the winter. One mile long, the trail takes you through pristine coastal
heathlands to a rise in the landscape for a lovely view toward Nantucket Sound
and Smith's Point. And the Maria Mitchell Association recommends an "early bird"
bird-watching ramble for this time of year.

Of course, if the weather is inclement or you're more in the mood to be pam-
pered, Nantucket offers world-class spa services at its perfect selection of elegant
hotels and inns. You'll be in fine form for dinner, dancing, and whatever else the
evening holds.

CRU, alas, is closed for the season. We are each celebrating New Year's Eve
quietly, at home, enjoying a decadent cozy dinner with loved ones and our favorite champagne. Here, in this closing chapter, we share with you our recipes for an
unforgettable dinner.

We hope we have given you a hundred reasons to make plans to visit the island
in the New Year. In the meantime, curling up with the *CRU Oyster Bar Nantucket
Cookbook* will be the next best thing. Cheers and happy New Year!

CAVIAR AND BLINIS

We love this recipe. The blinis are light and fluffy with crisp, buttery edges. While they make the perfect vehicle for caviar, they are equally delicious topped with smoked salmon or a little truffled egg salad. The list of options could go on and on . . . No matter which topping you use, the best accompaniment is always a glass of chilled champagne.

INGREDIENTS

½ teaspoon active dry yeast

¼ cup water, room temperature

¼ cup milk

1 tablespoon unsalted butter, plus extra for cooking the blinis

1 egg, separated

½ cup all-purpose flour

¼ cup buckwheat flour

½ teaspoon kosher salt

1 tablespoon olive oil or vegetable oil

2 ounces crème fraîche

Caviar

Sliced fresh chives

In a small bowl, dissolve the yeast in the water and set aside.

Warm the milk in a saucepan over low heat, add the butter and continue heating until the butter is melted; set aside to cool. Combine the milk and butter with the egg yolk and the water-yeast mixture.

Combine the flours and salt with the milk mixture. Transfer to a bowl, cover with plastic wrap, and set aside for 30 minutes to rise. (The recipe may be completed to this step and then refrigerated for a few hours until it is time to cook the blinis.)

Once the batter has risen and you are ready to cook the blinis, whisk the egg white until it forms soft peaks. Gently fold the whipped egg white into the batter.

(continued)

Warm a nonstick skillet over medium heat. Add ½ teaspoon of the oil and a tiny pat of butter to the pan. Drop 1-tablespoon portions of batter into the skillet and cook until golden brown on the first side. Flip and cook for another 30 to 60 seconds. Transfer the blinis to a platter, wipe out the pan, and repeat.

Top the warm blinis with crème fraîche and caviar and sprinkle some chives over the platter. Serve immediately.

OUR FAVORITE CHAMPAGNE PRODUCER: POL ROGER CHAMPAGNE

"My tastes are simple. I am easily satisfied with the best." So said the inimitable Winston Churchill. An enthusiastic fan of Pol Roger champagne and lifelong client of the Maison, he once described Pol Roger's headquarters in Epernay as "the world's most drinkable address." The admiration was mutual; in 1975 the company named a cuvee after him and in 2011, it renamed the street its headquarters sit on from Rue Henri Le Large to Rue Winston Churchill.

Epernay is the heart of France's champagne production and home to the most revered and well-known champagne houses in the world. The Pol Roger house has been part of that tradition since 1900, producing elegant wines that are sought after around the world. At CRU, we find the unique style of each Pol Roger wine makes a perfect pairing for our cuisine, which is why we always have it in stock. This is a champagne that complements perfectly the purity of our seafood and Chef Erin's classic yet innovative cooking style.

ROASTED OYSTERS WITH GARLIC AND PARSLEY BUTTER

Escargot butter, bourguignonne butter, maître d'hôtel butter—they are all ever so similar and delicious with oh-so many things. Butter infused with sweet garlic and lots of verdant parsley goes perfectly with anything including charred rib eye, land or sea snails, clams with pasta, or, as in this recipe, roasted oysters. You can make the butter well ahead of time and refrigerate or freeze it until you need it. Serve the oysters with a loaf of good, crusty bread.

INGREDIENTS

18 live oysters, shucked
Garlic and Parsley Butter (recipe follows)
1 lemon, cut in half

Preheat the broiler.

Place the oysters in a large cast-iron skillet. Top each oyster with 1 teaspoon of the garlic and parsley butter. Add the lemon halves to the pan, cut side up.

Broil the oysters 4 to 5 minutes, or until the bellies just begin to firm up and the outside of the oyster begins to ruffle.

Serve the oysters with the roasted lemon halves.

GARLIC AND PARSLEY BUTTER

→→ MAKES 6 OUNCES OF COMPOUND BUTTER ←←

INGREDIENTS

1 cup flat-leaf parsley leaves, finely chopped

2 shallots, finely chopped

6 garlic cloves, minced

½ cup (1 stick) unsalted butter, melted and hot, plus ½ cup
    (1 stick), cut into cubes and chilled

1 tablespoon grated lemon zest

¼ teaspoon kosher salt

Place the parsley, shallots, and garlic in a medium bowl. Pour
the hot melted butter over the chopped shallot mixture, stir
to combine, and let sit for a minute. Add the cubed cold
butter and stir vigorously to thoroughly combine. Stir in the
lemon zest and salt. Refrigerate or freeze the butter until
ready to use.

LOBSTER COCKTAIL

Dressed lobster is a special thing. Chilled and marinated with olive oil and citrus, the lobster is light, flavorful, and perfect for any occasion. It makes a great addition to a shellfish tower or as a light lunch at the beach.

INGREDIENTS

2 (1½-pound) live lobsters
½ fennel bulb, thinly sliced
8 kumquats, sliced and seeds removed, or 1 pink grapefruit,
    peeled and divided into segments
2 tablespoons extra-virgin olive oil
1½ tablespoons fresh lemon juice
1 tablespoon fresh tarragon leaves or flat-leaf parsley leaves
Flake sea salt

Place the lobsters in the bottom of a large stockpot with a tight-fitting lid. In a separate pot, bring 4 quarts of water to a boil. Pour the boiling water over the lobsters. Cover with the lid and leave undisturbed for 30 minutes. Remove the lobsters from the water and refrigerate.

When cooled, remove the lobster meat from the shells. Give the meat a quick rinse in cool water to be sure there are no shell fragments stuck to it; pat dry.

Remove and discard the intestine from the tails and cut the tails into bite-size pieces. Cut the claws in half. Place the lobster meat in a bowl and top with the fennel and kumquats. (At this point, the bowl may be covered and refrigerated for up to 1 hour or until ready to serve.)

Drizzle the oil and lemon juice over the lobster. Add the tarragon leaves and season with flake salt. Toss gently and serve.

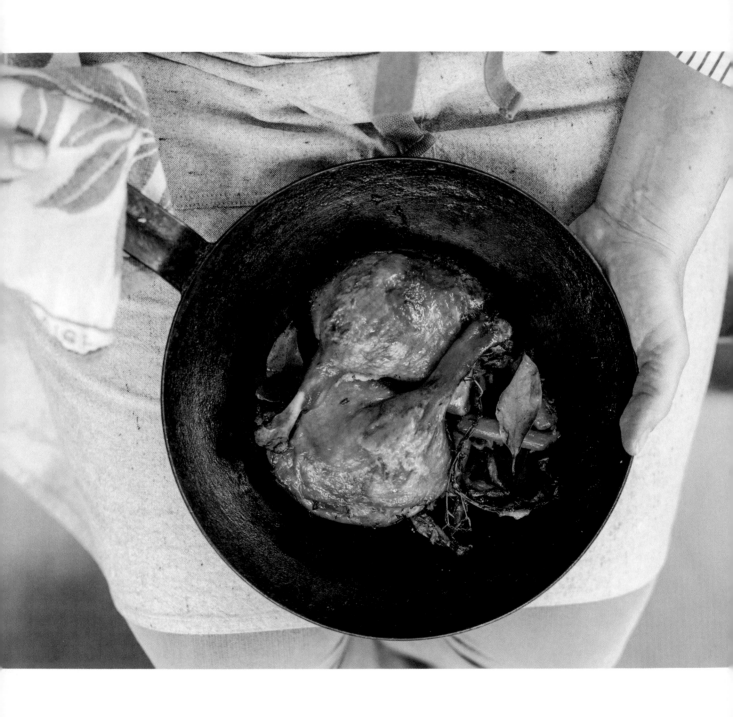

CONFIT-STYLE DUCK LEGS

→ **SERVES 4** ←

This recipe is a compilation of my mentors' various duck confit recipes with my favorite flavors added. The cure really penetrates and boosts the flavor of the duck, and braising the legs in wine instead of duck fat produces tender meat and a wonderful broth.

This dish is nicely complemented by a red wine from Napa, California: Sean Larkin's **Cabernet Franc**. Its notes of black fruit, chocolate, and licorice make this award-winning wine a showstopper—worthy of New Year's Eve and a hundred other occasions, too.

FOR THE CURE

2 tablespoons kosher salt
1 tablespoon sugar
4 garlic cloves
1½ teaspoons chopped fresh rosemary
½ teaspoon freshly ground black pepper
4 duck legs

FOR THE BRAISE

1 cup white wine
1 cup water
1 small white onion, sliced
1 carrot, peeled and chopped
2 sprigs fresh thyme
½ cinnamon stick
4 bay leaves
Kosher salt

TO CURE THE LEGS: Place the salt, sugar, garlic cloves, rosemary, and pepper in a food processor and pulse to combine. Rinse the duck legs under cool water and pat dry. Rub the flesh side of the duck with the spice mixture. Place the legs skin side up on a plate and refrigerate, uncovered, overnight.

TO BRAISE THE LEGS: The next day, bring the duck legs to room temperature. Preheat the oven to 325°F. Place the wine, water, onion, carrot, thyme, cinnamon stick, and bay leaves in a medium roasting pan or 12-inch cast-iron skillet; set the duck legs on top.

Cover tightly with foil and bake for 2½ hours. Uncover and carefully drain off just enough liquid to leave the flesh submerged and the skin dry.

Sprinkle the skin lightly with salt. Continue roasting, uncovered, for 30 minutes to brown and crisp the skin.

Serve the legs with bits of the roasted vegetables and some of the juices. Strain the remaining liquid and save it for the next time you make soup.

MACOMBER TURNIP AND BLACK TRUFFLE GRATIN

→ SERVES 6 ←

The Macomber turnips found at Bartlett's Farm in late fall are true heirloom turnips. John Bartlett Jr., whom everyone called June, began planting these turnips around 1910 and the seeds have been preserved each year since. This large, green-topped variety of turnip is incredibly sweet and versatile. They are terrific mashed, roasted, or pureed into soups. This recipe is rich and decadent. Perfect for a special holiday dinner.

INGREDIENTS

5 pounds Macomber turnips (or other green-topped turnips)

2 cups heavy cream

2 cups grated Comté cheese

2 ounces fresh black truffle, shaved

3 garlic cloves, finely chopped

1 tablespoon fresh thyme leaves

2 teaspoons kosher salt

¼ teaspoon grated nutmeg

Preheat the oven to 375°F. Butter a 12-inch gratin dish.

Peel the turnips and slice them into ¼-inch-thick slices. (This can be done with either a mandoline, a kitchen knife, or the slicing attachment on a food processor.) Layer the turnips in overlapping rows in the gratin dish.

In a bowl, stir together the cream, Comté, half the truffle, the garlic, thyme, salt, and nutmeg. Pour over the turnips. Cover the baking dish tightly with aluminum foil and bake for 45 minutes; the turnips will be tender at this point and most

(continued)

of the cream absorbed. Set the oven to broil, remove the aluminum foil, and finish the gratin under the broiler for 3 to 5 minutes to brown the top layer of turnips. Watch closely so it doesn't burn!

Sprinkle with the remaining truffle and serve.

NOTE: If fresh truffles are difficult to find, canned truffles or a little truffle oil can be substituted.

NANTUCKET WALKABOUT

to choose. The entire list of near-daily options includes each of Nantucket's protected lands, which are considerable, encompassing a variety of landscapes. You would need to spend weeks on the island to take them all in: Smith's Point, Sankaty Bluffs, Lost Farm Loop, Smooth Hummocks, and too many other walks to list await you. Check out a map and see which part of a place the Nature Conservancy has cited as "one of the last great places on earth" calls to you for a walkabout.

While you enjoy the pleasure of walking in the great outdoors taking in the beauty of the land and vistas, you'll be learning. Peter is a naturalist and published author and can tell you about the glacier that shaped Nantucket; how Nantucket got its unique collection of plants and wildlife; the marks left on the land by Native Americans and European settlers; contemporary conservation efforts; and a whole lot more. Each hike is part bird watching, part botany lesson, part geology class, and always, a glimpse into why Peter finds each exploration new and fascinating.

Select from a planned itinerary or talk with Peter about a customized walk. Sign up for a group hike if you enjoy meeting other travelers or reserve a private guided walk, for you and your family and friends only. And don't be surprised if, when your walk ends, you find yourself more in love with the island than ever. Peter's passion for the place is why he made Nantucket his year-round home twenty-five years ago.

There is no better way to get to know Nantucket island than on foot. Lucky for you, a guided hiking service, Nantucket Walkabout, is available year-round. The founder and lead guide, Peter Brace, leads two-hour walks winter, spring, summer, and fall, and offers a variety of itineraries from which

CHOCOLATE POTS DE CRÈME

This is one of our most beloved desserts at CRU. Creamy and decadent, it's like the richest chocolate pudding you've ever had—a perfect make-ahead dessert for the holidays or for a romantic Valentine's Day dinner.

Make the chocolate pots up to three days ahead, if you like. Keep the jars covered with plastic wrap in the refrigerator until ready to serve.

INGREDIENTS

10 ounces 60 percent bittersweet chocolate chips
12 egg yolks (freeze the whites for meringues)
⅔ cup sugar
1½ teaspoons sea salt, plus extra for sprinkling
4 cups heavy cream
1 cup whole milk
Whipped cream or dulce de leche

Preheat the oven to 325°F.

Place the chocolate in a large mixing bowl. In a separate bowl, whisk the egg yolks, sugar, and sea salt. Meanwhile, heat the heavy cream and milk over medium heat until very warm.

Pour half of the hot cream mixture over the chocolate; mix well. Slowly pour the other half over the sugar and egg yolks, whisking to keep the eggs from scrambling. Then add the egg mixture to the chocolate mixture and blend well.

Divide the pot de crème mixture among eight single-serving ramekins or custard cups. Place the ramekins in a roasting or baking pan and carefully pour in enough warm water to go halfway up the sides of the containers. Cover with aluminum foil and bake for 20 to 25 minutes or until they are set but still jiggle slightly in the middle. Remove the foil, transfer the pan to a wire rack, and let cool completely. Remove the cups from the roasting pan, cover with plastic wrap, and refrigerate at least two hours before serving.

Serve topped with lightly whipped cream and an additional sprinkle of sea salt.

A QUICK GUIDE TO THE RECIPES

While you will find a thorough index for each type of recipe and primary ingredient at the end of this book, we wanted to include a guide to the recipes by occasion—picnic fare, casual get-togethers around the grill, dinners at home, pull-out-all-the-stops entertaining, and so on—as well as by category to make it easy for you to design your own menus.

As you've noted by now, we arranged the chapters of this book to follow CRU's year—from our annual opening in the spring through the summer and into the fall, which marks the end of our official season. Then, we highlight Nantucket's delightful annual Holiday Stroll event, a long weekend in December when we reopen CRU for four days. In the final chapter we share our idea of the perfect New Year's Eve menu for an intimate dinner party.

Of course, regardless of how we have categorized any of the recipes here, it's your call as to how and when you want to serve them! And for drinks to accompany the food, you'll find our wine recommendations throughout this book as well as beer pairings, a collection of thirteen CRU cocktails, and eggnog. Cheers!

RECIPES BY CATEGORY

ABOUT
THE AUTHORS

Erin Zircher, Jane Stoddard, and Carlos Hidalgo

Erin Zircher is executive chef, cofounder, and proprietor of CRU Oyster Bar Nantucket. Her simple yet innovative cuisine, influenced by her classical French training and fondness for Mediterranean flavors, creates a culinary destination unmatched on Nantucket. The results have been featured in *Saveur*, *Town & Country*, and *Wine Spectator*.

During the off-season, she continues her exploration of food and wine by traveling. Recent destinations include Morocco; the Andalusia region of Spain; Sicily; the Calabria region of Italy; Burgundy, France; and Istanbul, Turkey.

Jane Stoddard, proprietor at CRU, says her primary focus is "ensuring that the customer experience at CRU is always exceptional." In the off-season, Jane enjoys exploring some of the world's most interesting culinary and wine regions. Those destinations include Spain, France, Morocco, Argentina, Mexico, Peru, and the Caribbean—all of them serving to inspire CRU's hospitality.

Carlos Hidalgo, proprietor of CRU, is responsible for its award-winning wine list and distinctive hand-crafted cocktail menu. A lifelong fascination with food and travel takes Carlos to wine and culinary regions across the world during CRU's off season—from Napa Valley to Argentina to Burgundy. A cheese aficionado, he enjoys hosting wine and cheese parties for friends.

Martha W. Murphy is an award-winning writer specializing in books about food, health, and business. She is glad to call New England "home," and deeply grateful to have had the help of Lucia Watson and Christine Madeira—two exceptional individuals—in the testing of these recipes.

ACKNOWLEDGMENTS

CRU continues to thrive and grow larger than we ever imagined because of the un-wavering support of our friends and family. They encourage us year after year. We are so happy to be able to share this book with our guests, whose loyalty helped create the experience CRU is today.

Thank you to our prestigious publisher, St. Martin's Press, and to senior editor BJ Berti and executive editor Elizabeth Beier, Macmillan executive vice president Steve Cohen, and editor in chief George Witte for believing in CRU and the stories we wanted to share.

Many thanks to our literary agent, Alan Morell, who has been a longtime advocate and patron. He guided us from day one to make this dream a reality. He allowed us to focus on highlighting the many facets of CRU while he focused on the business side of this project.

This project really found its wings with our coauthor and highly acclaimed writer, Martha W. Murphy, who worked tirelessly to capture the essence of four seasons of CRU.

Thank you to our CRU crew, who bring their passion and enthusiasm every day to make CRU the success it is today. We would not be the destination we are with-out their love and hard work.

It has been amazing to work with Wayne Chinnock for these gorgeous photo-graphs of CRU cuisine. His drive to capture all that we love about our little island thirty miles out to sea was invaluable.

We have been so fortunate to partner with our incredibly talented purveyors of pristine seafood, growers of gorgeous produce, and the makers of our most celebrated wines.

Lastly, this amazing Nantucket island community has embraced us with open arms from day one. We are so proud to call Nantucket our home.